With God on the Streets

The Robin Oake Story
Previously published as Gilbert Was Wrong!

Robin Oake

When Constabulary duty's to be done, to be done
A policeman's lot is not a happy one
The Pirates of Penzance – W.S. Gilbert

Authentic

16 15 14 13 12 11 10   8 7 6 5 4 3 2

First published in 2009 by Authentic Media
Reprinted 2010 by Authentic Media Limited
Milton Keynes
www.authenticmedia.co.uk

British Library Cataloguing in Publication Data
A catalogue record for this book is available from the
British Library

ISBN 978-1-85078-877-5

Cover Design by fourninezero design.
Printed and bound in Great Britain by J.F. Print, Sparkford

To my dear wife, Chris,
my late son Stephen,
his widow, Lesley
and
my daughters Judi and Sue
and their respective spouses and children.
You have all somehow loved, encouraged and
supported me,
often when I least deserved such affection. I
am so grateful.

Also to numerous former colleagues of all ranks,
many of whom
are part of this book.
Some have failed to get a mention and I apologise
for that
– it is mainly due to age and failing memory.
You are all appreciated.

Contents

Acknowledgements

I have had such a rewarding, sometimes exciting, always exhilarating career as a police officer that I feel I owe a debt of gratitude to those who encouraged me when I first felt drawn to the Metropolitan Police and to colleagues through the years – in whatever rank – with whom I have enjoyed working; also, to countless Christian friends who have prayed for me both generally and at specific times of challenge. For their patience, understanding, support and fellowship, I am deeply grateful.

I thank God especially for my close family – my parents; my two sisters, Cherry and Wendy, and their spouses John and David; for Chris, my lovely wife; my late son, dear Steve, and his cherished wife, Lesley; and my super daughters Judi and Sue and their husbands, Matthew and David. We also have some wonderful grandchildren who are so mature and doing well! I am indebted to pastors where I was in fellowship at Purley, Altrincham and Port St Mary for their teaching and trust.

I am also indebted to the Christian Police Association and its various directors – latterly George Roberts,

Harry Spain and Don Axcell; being an active and overt Christian is never an easy ride but it may be harder in the police service than in most professions. The CPA has been and still is a central and essential part of my life with the police.

So many friends have encouraged me to write this book, partly because of the humour involved but mostly because it traces a career of service to Her Majesty the Queen and her law-abiding subjects. These recollections are as accurate as a scrapbook has allowed me (though I apologise for any inaccuracies which might have occurred). I acknowledge the acceptance of the idea by Kath Williams, Editorial Coordinator at Authentic Media, and the tremendous expertise of editor Sheila Jacobs, who has been such a help with suggestions and revision of the script. There is by necessity much that has been omitted, so this book really just skims the surface of a fulfilled life which has given me so much pleasure, amongst the challenges. One of my tutors at police college commented that I had journalistic tendencies, but I do not believe that I am a natural author; however, although I hardly enjoyed writing my first book, *Father, Forgive*, this has been an enjoyable experience as I have relived my life in every rank from bottom to top, and asked myself the question once asked by a drunk in Moss Side: 'Did I do all that?'

Of all my acknowledgements, supremely I give thanks to our God and Father and to the Lord Jesus who saved me in my teenage years and whom I have endeavoured to serve since then, as the Holy Spirit has inspired, empowered and given me the strength to speak for him. My motivation has been to give all I have to him; in my service to others, I hope I have honoured him.

Foreword

Is it possible to combine sharp-end policing with adherence to strong Christian beliefs? Can a committed police officer also be a strongly committed Christian? Can society, in general terms, reconcile the concepts of forgiveness and retribution? How can we define 'Justice' in the modern day?

All of these issues, and more, are implicit and integral in this illuminating and essentially very human story of endeavour, success and family tragedy – told with classical simplicity by the author who, more than most has seen life in all its contrasting shades from London's West End and back streets to the top tables of a major industrial city. They are all there – Royalty, politicians, fake Archbishops, call-girls, petty thieves, terrorist bombs, high society and low society – a rich and illuminating tapestry. And this may not be the half!

Robin Oake speaks of his experience in several testing police environments; across London, in Manchester and finally commanding the police on the Isle of Man. His strong Christian faith is central to his philosophy of life. It fortified his approach to many challenges that he had to confront and we see how it supported him throughout his rich and varied career.

The murder of his son Stephen, when serving as a detective in Manchester, is touched upon here only briefly (see Robin's other book *Father Forgive*) but it shocked the nation. The circumstances lifted a lid on the dangerous world of terrorism, organised crime and illegal immigration yet, throughout, Robin and his family ride above the ensuing tide of public outrage and recrimination. Many will remember their calmness and forgiveness at that time, which was inspirational.

Robin Oake's story, and that of his constantly supportive family, is told here with humility, pride and much humour! It is an example to us all; a rare insight into the day-by-day work of a Service that stands centrally in our society and is essential to maintain our favoured way of life.

Lord Dear, Willersey, Gloucestershire,
lately H.M. Inspector of Constabulary

GLOSSARY

It might be of some use to you, the reader, to glance through this glossary of terms (especially if you are not a police officer!) as pertained to the Metropolitan Police 1957 to 1978.

Board: Promotion selection panel of senior officers
Bramshill: International Police Staff College in Hampshire
Cards: System of regularly checking licensed premises
CO: Commissioner's Office (New Scotland Yard)
Commissioners: On the Isle of Man, local councillors
CPA: Christian Police Association
Districts: Four districts (incorporating six divisions) in the Met with Commander rank in charge
Divisions: Areas titles A to Z (except I and Q) with Chief Superintendent in charge
Duty Board: Assignments to constables for their shift (parading up to fifty constables)
High Bailiff: Senior magistrate
House of Keys: On the Isle of Man, the lower House of Tynwald (parliament)
Information Room: Central communications room with radio to units

Juvenile Bureau: Specialist police unit dealing with juvenile offenders

Mad Sunday: The middle Sunday of the two-week TT meeting, so-called because of the madness of the motorcyclists on the open roads

Manx Grand Prix: Motorcycle races for amateurs on TT course

MHK: Member of the House of Keys

Police house: Married quarters supplied by police

Police Orders: Twice weekly update of staff changes and legislation

Police Review: Publication for all police forces with news, comment and senior staff changes

Relief: A group of shift officers.

Section House: Police accommodations for single men or women

Speaker in the House of Keys is the equivalent to the Speaker in the House of Commons

TT races: Tourist Trophy Motor Cycle Races founded in 1907

Introduction

So many people, when asking me to speak at various functions, want to know about my background, my wife, my family, the various jobs I did while in the police service, what I do in my spare time and so on that I felt I must try to put it all into order. Then, when I am asked again, all I shall have to say is 'Why don't you read my book?'!

I have tried to balance the sadder aspects of policing with humour, for I really do believe – contrary to the opinion of W.S. Gilbert – that a policeman's lot is indeed a happy one. However, I have frequently been asked whether the murder of my Special Branch son, Stephen, in Manchester has affected my view that policing is a great vocation and is, generally, 'a happy lot'. I haven't changed my mind on that – he was immersed in and enjoyed his work, as did I; we both knew the risks and, while the family and I miss him so much, my overall view has not been altered.

Obviously, there are things I have been involved in during my police career that cannot be fully told in a book. But I hope the flavour of my outlook in life and what it is that keeps me so optimistic and joyful comes through. So you will not read great detail about the murders, rapes, fires, serious accidents, demonstrations and firearms incidents with which I have had to deal. If I dwelt on those, I might have agreed that a policeman's lot is *not* very happy – although it was the life I expected when I joined. No, these pages are about great memories, fulfilment, many good colleagues who became firm friends – and a sense of humour. It is also the story of a Christian police officer who has found a strong faith which has sustained him, and his family, through testing times.

And now, I invite you to read on and see if you agree with me that Gilbert was wrong!

Robin Oake
Autumn, 2008

1.

Early days

When my eldest sister, Cherry, was promised a real, live pet for her seventh birthday, 28 June 1937, she let Mother and Dad know she wanted a tortoise. Her mind was set on it. She told her friends about it and the box she had made for it to sleep in. True, Cherry wondered why her mother had gone into hospital some days before the present was due, but was whooping with delight when she heard that Mother was coming home on her birthday.

'Look, darling!' said Mum, showing Cherry a 22-inch long bundle. 'Your birthday present – a brother!'

'Oh no!' wailed Cherry. 'You promised me a tortoise!'

She obviously got used to the idea – in time – and she, my other sister, Wendy, and I all grew up together. Actually, I was a 'mistake', but finding this out didn't shock or upset me at all; we were a close-knit and generally very loving family.

Father's line was in carpentry – his father and grandfather were actually in the trade. When pushed, Dad eventually let us know the family secret: his eighteenth- and nineteenth-century ancestors were convicted smugglers in Rye, Sussex. He took me to see their graves at St Mary's

Church. It was a little eerie to see the smugglers name –
Oake – etched into the gravestones.

In those days, we lived in a smallish three bedroom
detached house in Hooley, near Couldson, Surrey. There
was no central heating so, on many winter mornings, we
would wake to icy windows.

I was only two-and-a-quarter when World War Two
broke out. We had an Anderson shelter built in 1941 in
the back garden, not five yards from the kitchen. I
remember standing in the garden, watching small aero-
planes swooping and diving somewhere to the north of
us and I was told that it was the Battle of Britain –
Spitfires and Hurricanes against the deeper engine noise
of the German planes. One day, we had a visit from
Charlie Glass, an old colleague of Dad's, who suggested
we all had a picnic. We'd go in his car to Kingswood
Golf Course to watch the dogfights in the air. We sat at
the edge of the course and, through binoculars, had an
excellent view. Then came a shout: 'Quick! Come on!
Under the trees!' My parents were yelling and shouting
as Charlie Glass dragged me away – I wanted to stay
and watch what was happening! A plane, smoking from
its wings, was diving straight for the course and it
crashed about 200 yards from us.

Dad and Charlie carefully made their way to the
German plane which was now burning fiercely; they
could see no pilot and, before long, two fire engines
arrived with the Home Guard making sure than none of
us got too close. What excitement.

My father originally worked with the General Post
Office (telephones), having gone direct from technical
college into the workplace as an apprentice. In fact, he
won a competition before he was married to design
what was then thought impossible – an automatic telephone exchange. His design won him five shillings, a

congratulatory handshake from his boss – and nothing else. If only he had patented the idea! However, he rose through the ranks and by the time war broke out, he had become part of the management. He was called up for the forces and drafted into the Royal Electrical and Mechanical Engineers as a junior officer before that posting was cancelled as he was deemed an essential worker. Not long after, he was sent to deal with telecommunications in the 'underground' cabinet office off Horse Guards Road in London. Here he spent the rest of the war alongside people such as Winston Churchill and General Eisenhower. We saw little of him though he occasionally came home for a few days on leave.

It was while he was home and asleep upstairs on the morning of 7 July 1944 – my mother's birthday – that tragedy struck. It was a Saturday and lunch was being prepared in the kitchen; I was with my sisters at the front of the house with our next-door neighbour's son, David Dickenson. He had piled tea chests on top of each other and we would climb up and, with a telescope, watch the doodlebugs fly over, en route, presumably, to London. We all knew the risks – one of these flying bombs had a matter of seconds to crash-land and explode once their engine had cut out.

Then it happened. David was up top, a plane was coming towards us and wow! its engine cut out. Not a plane at all – a flying bomb! We screamed for Mum to get out of the house and we all dived into the Anderson shelter, just slamming the door as an almighty explosion blew it back in on us, showering us with debris. We discovered that the bomb had landed on some houses opposite, completely demolishing them; two ladies were killed. Of course, we didn't know that at the time; spitting dust and dirt, Mother was first up, clambering out, yelling for Dad. He had been in bed. But there wasn't much of our house intact . . .

In fact, an inexplicable miracle had happened – in his sleep, Dad had imagined that he heard a doodlebug's engine cut out. He had leapt out of bed, jumped down the stairs and dived under the Morrison shelter (a steel table we had had installed some time earlier). As he crawled out, he faced Mother, bleeding badly from a cut on his forehead.

As a result of this, we were all looked after by other neighbours that day. Then we stayed in what was known as 'the deep shelter' dug into the hills in the grounds of Cane Hill Hospital, Coulsdon – dank, dripping and crowded out. Thank God, Auntie Bell, in Poole, Dorset, offered to accommodate us (except for Dad who went back to work in the cabinet rooms). So the rest of us set off by train for a year away from Hooley.

For a young lad, it was a superb place to be: a naval base, with minesweepers and motor torpedo boats and, even better, Sunderland flying boats in the harbour in front of Brownsea Island – and holidays for a month before going to Longfleet School with Wendy, while Cherry travelled to Parkstone Grammar.

So we watched the war from a distance . . . the troop build-up in Dorset and Devon, increased exercises, practise landings on the shores . . . the downside was seeing ships returning to base, damaged, some with canvas wraps round bodies, and the sound of the lone trumpet on the quayside as they were carried ashore in Poole – a sound which still haunts me today.

We made some good friends in Dorset, enjoyed school and sport but missed Dad. He was in the thick of it in London and he couldn't communicate with us often because of the secrecy of his workplace. Even after the war (and until he died) he rarely spoke about his experiences.

When the war had ended we arrived back in Surrey; the house had been repaired, the houses opposite were being rebuilt, and we had, for the first time I could remember, a holiday. Again, thanks to relations, we took over a house in Greatstone, Kent. It was virtually on the beach behind the sand dunes.

I recall the day we went to Dungeness by train specifically to climb the lighthouse. It was daunting since the steps were built inside the tall 'tube'; going up was nerve-racking but going down . . . I looked at these narrow, worn steps and was choked with fear. I just could not move. My sisters bravely turned their backs on the steep steps and, one by one, coaxed me down. I was speechless, shaking with fright and very ashamed. When we reached the bottom, my first reaction was simple 'I don't like heights; I'll never do anything like that again.' But as I got over the shock, I knew I did not want to grow up afraid of heights so I determined to overcome the phobia. At first, I would climb a stepladder, then a longer ladder; I would volunteer to clean out the gutters at home for Dad; at a building site I would, when the workmen had gone home, climb scaffolding. In fact, as the next couple of years came and went, I must have climbed anything possible above the ground to overcome this fear. To be honest, even now on very high platforms or in a cable car my stomach may turn but, while I respect safety for height, I can overcome the fear. I am so glad that I did overcome the phobia, as there were many occasions during my career when heights just had to be mastered.

Around this time, I was beginning to take a real interest in sport. Dad would sometimes take me to Stamford Bridge to watch his beloved Chelsea. At Chipstead Primary School, we played soccer in the winter and cricket in the summer. We were fortunate that Mr J.B.

Stoddart, a retired professional cricket coach from Harrow School spent much time with us.

At Chipstead Cricket Club, I was very fortunate to know Charlie Gasson who was a tenor in the church choir as well as the Second XI captain. One day in the vestry as we were putting on our robes, he took me aside and asked me if I would like to learn how to score for cricket. I somehow got the hang of this complicated task and, aged about ten or so, became the scorer for the Second XI side. Cheeky as I was, I would turn up to practise in the nets – only to watch, of course, and then hope to get a bat or a bowl when most of the good players had gone into the bar. Then, one day as I was batting in the dusk, a man named Colin Dunkeld asked me where I had learnt my cricket. When I mentioned the school coach, his eyebrows lifted and the very next week I was asked if I wanted to join in the adult practice in the nets.

Then it happened; someone didn't turn up for our match away at South Nutfield. Charlie Gasson asked, 'Got your gear, Robin? Want a game?'

First ball . . . I stepped down the wicket and hit it over the bowler's head for six! I went on to score thirty-six not out and was so embarrassed when the team came out of the pavilion and stood to clap me in. That began a few years of cricket with Chipstead, mostly in the Second XI and occasionally in the First – if they couldn't get someone to turn out on a Bank Holiday!

2.

The beginning of the rest of my life

On Sundays, we went to church – Cherry, Wendy and me. (Sometimes Mother would come, but rarely; Dad always cooked the Sunday lunch.) The three of us sang in the choir.

We more or less ran a 'book' on which sermon the rector would preach so there would be a softened cheer in the choir-stalls when we got it right. We guessed that the rector had just 104 sermons in his notebook which got him through the fifty-two weeks of the year, two services each Sunday. Presumably he had some others for weddings and funerals.

On Sunday afternoons, it was Sunday school. My last day in that Sunday school – the years I had attended did very little for me – was completely unplanned but actually was the beginning of the rest of my life. The girl in front of me had long plaits which tickled my knees when we were sitting down. I had a superb idea which took some skill in its execution. I knew that if I tied her plaits in a knot to the back of her tubular green chair, it would cause quite a distraction when she stood up to sing.

Have you ever tried to tie plaits? It's difficult to do without the person knowing what is going on – but I managed it!

Then it happened. Success! As she stood up to sing, the chair lifted with her. She screamed, and the chair banged down with her on it. I wasn't very popular with the teachers although I was cheered by my mates as I was dismissed.

My very happy days at Chipstead County Primary School had come to an end. I had passed the 11+ examination, and went to Reigate Grammar School, teaming up with my long-time friend, Bob Barkway. Of course, we now had homework. I wasn't a natural student though I hope I was conscientious enough to do my best in what work was set, though I doubt if I went the extra mile. I suppose I was an all-rounder – not outstanding at anything but holding my own in the middle of the pack.

I mentioned that leaving Sunday school was really the beginning of the rest of my life. Despite my parents 'lapsed Free Church' stance, they still wanted us to go to church. So let me go back a bit. I may be one of the few people in life who actually remembers his christening and was slightly embarrassed by the whole palaver. Cherry was persuaded that she ought, at the age of thirteen, to be confirmed but there was a problem – she had not been christened. Neither had Wendy, now aged eight, nor me, aged six. So the day came when we all gathered at the font in Chipstead Church – including parents, godparents and friends. Cherry was subsequently confirmed, as were Wendy and I some time later.

Meanwhile, some of Cherry's friends went to Purley Girl Crusader Class on Sunday afternoons, so she left the Sunday school. When my moment of shame came, it was discovered that there was a Boy Crusader Class, also in Purley. A friend invited me along. I had heard that in addition to the 'religious' bit, they had woodworking evenings, sports days, inter-class outings and annual camps and house parties.

That summer, I had been entered for the 440 yards (roughly 400 metres) under-thirteens, at the Crusader Sports at Motspur Park. Through a heat and a semi-final, I found myself lining up for what to me was a very gruelling race. I was first at the tape by a good margin, and the All-England Crusader Junior Champion. I received a chrome spoon and was thrilled. Then at the school sports, I won the Victor Ludorum Junior Cup having won the 100 and 220 yards races and being second in the Long Jump. After a good summer, it was an introduction to rugby. I wasn't sure that I wanted to play this weird game of handling and running with an oval ball. As with cricket, rugby was played midweek and on Saturday mornings; so my friend Bob and I found ourselves in the Junior XV playing rugger in the morning and football for Reigate Rovers in the afternoon.

The second part of what I mean by 'the beginning of the rest of my life' was to happen in my early teens through Crusaders – and not the sport. It began after Cherry, home on summer break from Nonington College of Physical Education near Canterbury, Kent, announced at a meal one evening, 'I've become a Christian.'

You could have heard a pin drop. We were all there eating our beans on toast – then, a pregnant silence. I think it was Mum who said, 'What do you mean? You go to church. You were already a Christian.'

Cherry then told us that she had asked Jesus into her life. Of course this was all new to us; that sort of thing never seemed to be talked about at church, though I did vaguely remember some mention of it at Crusaders on a

Sunday afternoon. What was obvious, though, was that Cherry had something indescribable about her which indicated a real change. Whatever it was, it began to permeate the whole household. One of the things that happened – and not exactly welcomed at the time – was that Cherry would come to my room to read the Bible and pray with me.

I was due to go to Crusader Camp at Studland Bay in Dorset in August 1950 – returning to territory which I knew well from the war days. I had persuaded my friend Bob to come too and it was a thoroughly good and exciting ten days in great summer weather. I enjoyed playing 'halo' (a derivative of hoopla – throwing a hoop across a net and scoring like badminton) and, with the officer who had asked me to partner him playing doubles, won the final in the week-long tournament. What really impressed me, however, was not all the great outdoors stuff but the evening sessions in the marquee. Our padre was from the Africa Inland Mission. He was my picture of a missionary – short, dumpy, glasses like the bottom of milk bottles, shorts that were too long, and so correct – and yet he was dynamic with his talks based on the Bible.

Towards the end of the week, I was moved enough to speak with him after one of those sessions and enquire how I could become a Christian. It had never been explained to me even at church or Sunday school – at least, not that I could remember. With the speaker, I went to the commandant's tent – Kenneth Anderson, a bridge designer amongst other things – and we talked through my way of life, my sin, why Jesus had died on the cross, and how I could become a Christian and actually receive Jesus into my life. I really wanted this to happen. We knelt by the upside-down tea chest in that tent and I prayed, asking Jesus to forgive my sin and to come into my heart. I was moved to tears. I had become a Christ follower. Next day, Cherry made a surprise visit. Thrilled to hear what I had done, she said, 'Now you're truly my brother', which took some understanding.

Soon after this, Tom Rees, the evangelist from Hildenborough Hall, Kent, conducted a mission in Redhill, Surrey. Cherry, Wendy and I attended. Many people went forward for counselling at the end of the evening, including Wendy, who also became a Christian then.

It was in 1954 that Billy Graham came to London amid much publicity, with his three-month long crusade at Harringay Arena. There was a lot of excitement and razzmatazz and, sometime during that period, we went with Mother up to London and to the crusade. The atmosphere was something of which we knew nothing in our church – wonderful choir, great music. After Billy had preached, hundreds of people got up out of their seats and went forward to meet with counsellors. Mother went, too, and was converted. When this news reached Dad he confessed to being a backslider and so both my parents got right with God. At last, we were a Christian family together.

The immediate effect was that Cherry started a Bible study group once a week at home – she was now teaching in Guildford. It grew to about fifty people of all ages coming together without any denominational bias to study and discuss God's Word. It was a great help to us all. In fact, from this, I was invited to attend Purley Baptist Church, and from that, asked to join the local Lay Preachers Association. I was patiently taught and nurtured by Keith Stockbridge and Ray Burgess and eventually given full responsibility to take a complete service on my own in Norwood, south London. Cherry came to support me for that first 'solo' service. I even remember my first sermon – from Psalm 92:12: 'The righteous will flourish like a palm tree' (NIV).

Soon, the Methodist Church in Coulsdon asked if they could have a service each Sunday evening in the Hooley Community Centre. Dad and Mother offered to help there and so a missionary work in Hooley was begun! Things were really happening in the Oake family.

I want to place on record how much my parents were appreciated by my sisters and me. Despite the war years and the sparse resources, our parents did their utmost to keep a happy, well-disciplined household. We never missed out at Christmas – often our father would hand-make toys and somehow ensure that coloured lights, home-made crackers and filled stockings were all part of the festivities. He would 'blow' chickens' eggs and fill them solid with chocolate. He never did pass on the secret of how that was done! They encouraged us with our homework, our sport, our hobbies; they were only cross when we did something wrong and while we may not have appreciated the punishment at the time, we were soon forgiven and restored. Dad had, from my earliest memories, spent much time with me. I do hope that some of the affection which so encouraged me was passed on to Steve, our son, and from him to his own son, Christopher.

3.

Changes

I'd enjoyed being in the Combined Cadet Force at school with its summer camps, and all the sport, but at the age of sixteen I was unsure of the direction I wanted to take in life after school. I had thought of a life in sport but was discouraged because, in those days, there were very few professional positions; I thought of following Dad into a technical job but he had ended his career in an office, so I was deterred; I thought of the Royal Navy, and its engineering branch. In the May of my GCE year, I took the examination to enter the Naval College at Rosyth. I passed and had a successful medical in the Strand, London. Mother was not keen on my leaving home, or the Royal Navy. Dad, very sensibly, sat me down to talk the whole thing through.

'Now are you absolutely sure? You're sixteen now but from the blurb I see that you'll have to sign on for twelve years from your eighteenth birthday – that's fourteen years of your life. Do you *really* want that?'

This was a life-changing time. We didn't stop talking until well into the night. And I decided it was not what I wanted after all.

So GCEs came and went and I decided not to go on to sixth form. Dad discovered there was a civil service exam in July. I sat that with the thought that I would have to do National Service when I reached eighteen so I could be paid for nearly two years, do the two years in the services and in those four years, discover what I really wanted to do in life.

It was at about this time that one or two friends at the home Bible study group wondered if I was involved with a youth club at Chipstead Church. Apart from maybe four or five others of my age, there were precious few to call a club of any sort. So, arranging for someone else to ring my bell once or twice on a Sunday evening, I cycled with Clyde Quiney to Purley to attend the Baptist Church, where there was a packed congregation, few formalities and a great girl who was wearing a red fez on her head and who winked at me from the choir. After the dynamic service, I was surrounded by other young people who wanted to know who I was and where I was from and 'What about coming to Christian Endeavour on Tuesday?' I was reeling from the enthusiasm; immediately hooked, I wanted to get stuck in. My loyalties were still with Chipstead but I plucked up courage and spoke with the rector about leaving. He was very gracious and once I had shelved my bell-ringing duties I hived off to Purley each week, morning and evening, and on Tuesday evenings.

I found myself talking to a young lady at Christian Endeavour – about my age, full of fun, well-built, great smile – and a wicked wink. Ah, the girl in the choir!

'What's your name?' I asked.

'Christine Murray.'

I wanted to get to know her but was seeing someone else. Still, God was moving in a mysterious way.

I passed the civil service exam and was offered a position as a clerical officer in the Prison Commission and duly reported to Horseferry House, Dean Ryle Street, London, SW1 in September – the commission's headquarters. Two years later, I had the call-up papers, as predicted, and duly arrived at the army recruiting office for the six-point medical. Although I should have expected this appointment with Her Majesty's Forces, I was more than a little miffed as I had just been selected as goalkeeper for the Home Office soccer team. Nevertheless, with my running in the mornings and the weekly games, I was fit and well so I felt that the medical was a formality. Fit? Fit for nothing – or so it seemed. Some weeks later a green card was posted through our front door to starkly say without any explanation that I was medically unfit for National Service. My parents sought an answer as to why. The War Office would not yield any information and our local GP could find nothing wrong, so he made arrangements for us to see a specialist in Harley Street. For two days I was poked and pulled, scrutinised and listened to, giving specimens of this and that. At the end of it all, the senior man said, 'Robin, there's nothing wrong with you except that your feet are too big for army boots!'

So, I was back at Horseferry House. A bonus of working in Dean Ryle Street was that I was able to regularly see Chris – who by now, after a few hiccoughs, was my girlfriend – as she travelled from the nurses' home in Chelsea across to St Thomas's Hospital.

Cherry – now a well established gym-mistress at Pewley School in Guildford – began to ask me if I had ever sought to seek God's plan for my life. She reminded me that God says to us all, 'I know the plans I have for you . . . plans to prosper you and not to harm you, plans to give you hope and a future' (Jer. 29:11, NIV).

I must have read these verses from the Old Testament but had not taken in the significance. Cherry's counsel was that 'If God knows the plan for your life, why not get in touch by prayer and ask him what it is?' I'd never thought of that.

So she and I sometimes prayed together and I certainly prayed earnestly because of this unexpected two-year gap. I was still in the Prison Commission, and had worked in Wandsworth Prison and Feltham Borstal; I was regularly reading reports from various establishments in the land where men and women were incarcerated, including police reports. At home, I was reading the family's edition of the *Christian Herald* and was startled by an advertisement seeking men and women for the Metropolitan Police. In the *Christian Herald*? I had been praying for some sort of leading towards a job, and was slightly despondent that nothing had come up – I was even thinking about training to be a prison governor – when this notice strangely warmed my heart. A police officer? The interesting reports; the outside life; the various skills within policing; it was intriguing. In my naivety, I hadn't realised that if I was promoted above inspector, I would be driving a desk again.

'Ah,' I said to myself, 'Stuart McInnes is a police constable. He's at church occasionally. I'll have a word with him.' When I did, he encouraged me and I felt that God was in this but had to test it. Remember, I was medically unfit for the British Army so I figured that if I passed a police medical that would be the real indication that it was the right career. I remember thanking God for this new direction and was confident that all would be well.

Just after the rugger season had finished in April, I had an answer from the application which accompanied my short CV. It was to attend for interview and medical at Beak Street Recruiting Centre just off Regent Street in

London. I took a day's annual leave from my prison job and, smartly dressed in a suit, attended as requested. The written test was fine, the interview with three senior officers daunting but not too demanding, and then the medical . . . a doctor in a white coat met me in a well-equipped room, asked me about my being medically unfit for the army, and I was put through a series of tests – and pronounced A1 fit. At the end of the day, I heard my name being read out as successful. I was to be a policeman.

I got home as soon as I could – no mobiles in those days to ring the news through. I got a mediocre welcome from my mother ('What if you're attacked? It's too dangerous!'). When Dad came home some time later, he was thrilled. He wanted to know all about it; he wanted to read the literature that I had brought with me, and I felt a stronger bond than ever with him. I have to say that Mother came round to the idea fairly soon after, Dad reassuring her that this was God's way.

A week later I had a letter from the Metropolitan Police (the first time that I had had an envelope addressed to R.E.N. Oake Esq – I felt really proud) asking me to report to Peel House Training Centre, Regency Street, Pimlico, London on Monday 24 June 1957 at 8.30 a.m. – this was six weeks away, enabling me to give the full month's notice to the Prison Commission.

I had many good colleagues at Horseferry House but it was Bob End I missed the most. He was a Christian; we often lunched, took walks along the Embankment, prayed and studied the Bible together. He was such an encourager and teacher. A former station sergeant from the Metropolitan Police was also working in the Prison Commission and he gave me much advice in those last days there, one piece which has remained with me ever since: 'Robin, never lose your sense of humour.'

My friends at church were all excited about my becoming a police officer. At the evening service on Sunday 23 June, a number of people prayed for me and gave me a good send-off. Immediately after that service, Cherry took me to a gymnast friend of hers in Purley whose husband was a police officer in Croydon – both Christians whom I had never met. Olive and Ron Perrett welcomed me in; we talked at length, both of them contributing anecdotes and advice before we all knelt in their small front room to pray together. Ron Perrett advised me, 'Nail your colours to the mast, Robin!' – meaning not to be shy about admitting I was a Christian. Nervous though I was about this new beginning, I was elated that so many had given this prayer support for what I expected to be a demanding training period and career ahead.

4.

Training

On Monday 24 June 1957, aged nineteen and 364 days, I became Police Constable 711TS at Peel House, one of two Metropolitan Police training schools, and began a career which ultimately spanned forty-two years.

I was ushered in with nineteen other slightly nervous fellow recruits to be fitted with uniforms. I spent the first evening doing nothing but ironing and spit and polishing – with much help from Gordon Humble, a recently retired Guards sergeant.

Peel House was an old building in Regency Street, SW1 and was a police training establishment long before Hendon was established. Sleeping accommodation consisted of two long dormitories on two floors, segmented into twenty-five 'rooms' either side of a long, narrow corridor. The 'rooms' contained a bed, chair, table with two drawers, and hooks on the wall and on the back of the door. By standing up, one could see along the dorm and there was a six-inch gap at the bottom so the partition between each room was about six foot in length and the room itself about eight foot by six.

My daily routine was always to kneel by my bed to read the Bible and pray before sleeping. On this first night and within seconds of kneeling down, my door was thrust open with my new neighbour yelling, 'What the hell do you think you're doing? Err . . . oh!' My feet were under the partition and in his segment! He apologised; he was as embarrassed as I was. But it didn't take long for the news to get round the intake that I was religious – the expression used by one of the class was that I had 'a tile loose'.

Still, we soon all settled in together. There was inspection early next morning and our first time on parade, then the swearing-in and promise of loyalty to our Queen. Chief Superintendent Miller – tall, bald and smart in his uniform – conducted this ceremony and gave us a few words of advice, some of which I remembered and often repeated to myself and other recruits: 'You have joined the police service; I emphasise the word "service" since you will principally be serving Her Majesty and her subjects. You will never be rich financially but you will have a life of rich experience. Most of you will remain in the most important rank of constable. Rank would bring privilege but not dominance. You are still a servant of the public. One final thing – if you have a sense of humour don't lose it; if you don't have any humour get some quickly. I wish you the best of luck.' Humour again!

At six foot five, I was naturally given the nickname 'Lofty' from the broken-nosed Drill Sergeant Castle. First time away from home that it was, I was perfectly happy doing something with a challenge and a future. Big Brian Eales (six foot seven and twenty-three stone) sought me out and introduced me to the Christian Police Association which then met in Vauxhall Bridge Road. George Paisley was the general secretary and when I met him he said, rather brusquely, 'You'll be giving your testimony when I call on you.' So with about ten days' police service, here I was speaking to men and women, many double my age and some with rank . . . but it was a great start to see a good number of Christian police officers meeting together.

One lasting memory of training school was the senior stage under the then Station Sergeant Goulding (who rose to the rank of Commander). He was a great teacher, but one Saturday morning he wrote on the board the word 'Riots', wrote the paragraphs we should read on the subject and then announced, 'Riots are a thing of the past; you'll not meet any in your service so instead of an hour's lesson, we'll have a test!'

Within two months, I was bussed to Notting Hill for . . . a riot! Then, soon after, I was at the centre of the Camden Town rent riots – we arrived in a police car to have our way blocked by an upturned trolleybus and, in the melee, one of my colleagues was killed by a washing machine which had been hurled from a top-floor balcony. Later, as a sergeant, I was in Red Lion Square, central London, at what was meant to be a peaceful demonstration but turned nasty to the point that a student, with 'Ban the Bomb' on his T-shirt, was killed. Again, as a sergeant, I was in Grosvenor Square when a demonstration against Americans in Vietnam turned sour and a riot ensued. I was at the American airbase at Uxbridge at least once a month as part of the thin blue line preventing demonstrators from gaining entrance by fair means or (mostly) foul.

Some years later, and I was an inspector then, I was in charge of two sergeants and twenty PCs guarding the Cenotaph during a rampage in Whitehall when thirteen burning coffins were hurled at the door and walls of 10 Downing Street. This riot was solely to do with the military and an operation months before in Londonderry when thirteen civilians were killed by gunfire. In

Whitehall, thousands of 'uncontrollables' were hurling bricks, sticks and using various weapons against the police – in fact, an unknown inspector, bleeding from a facial wound, came to seek refuge with my men on the Cenotaph and as he turned with relief, a half paving stone flew through the air like a flying saucer, took his cap, ripped it off with only the peak remaining, and flew on into the crowd. He could have been killed had the missile been an inch or so lower. Reinforcements arrived soon after that with – who at the front? Commander Goulding! Even in the noise he grinned as I yelled to him, 'No riots in my time?'

Following my introduction to the International Christian Police Association (as it was then) I was regularly invited to join Ron Perrett, Jim Green, Frank Lording, Bryan Eales, Horace Elphick (former Chief Inspector), Graham Bailey and others – shift duties permitting – to participate in church services, mostly at small gospel halls. I was later to meet 'Uncle' John – that is, John Williamson, former Chief Constable of Northampton Police and the president of ICPA. His pet phrase was 'I joined the police fearing God and the sergeant; I left fearing only God!' The secretary of the association, you remember, was George Paisley. They were all great encouragers to me. The police service can be a difficult and sometimes lonely place for an active Christian, but the fellowship of men and women who are followers of Christ is so rewarding.

At an early stage in my career, Chris gave me a pocket-size Bible. Without any exception and in every rank, I always carried it in my left breast pocket, along with a New Testament elsewhere; these were very well used, especially on duty – maybe simply for personal reading, helping people in grief when they asked me or, occasionally, using scripture to introduce a colleague or someone with whom I have had to deal to the Lord Jesus. Despite my early keenness – and perhaps over-enthusiasm – to always look to speak about the hope that I have as a Christian, I was always very careful not to intrude or force the issue and, sensibly, never to speak about it when I should be doing other things on duty. Having said that, I would – if acting as jailer – often put a tract on the food tray or take the opportunity to listen and talk with prisoners, again without forcing my faith on any of them. Incidentally, that pocket Bible might have been small but I can remember several occasions when it prevented serious injury. By being in my pocket it took the brunt of, for instance, a blow with a scaffold pole from a violent man whom I was attempting to arrest; and there was the mental patient wielding a chisel which went through the pocket and stopped, fortunately, on the cover. Then, as Superintendent in Manchester, in a street melee, severe punches were stopped by the world's bestseller in my left breast pocket.

My first contact with St John Ambulance was at the Metropolitan Police training school, since all recruits were instructed in first aid and it was imperative that every officer passed the examination. This introduction and continuation throughout my forty-two years of police service culminated later as a council member then Commander of the Isle of Man St John Ambulance and the chapter delegate of the Order of St John in London. I was very glad to have the training as even then, one could envisage the need for first aid on the beat in a multitude of situations.

In the last week of the senior stage, with practical tests and a written examination, I passed and was second in the class behind my good friend David Polkinghorne (who later became a Commander in the Metropolitan Police but sadly died prematurely); the postings were read out and John Day (later a Detective Chief Superintendent), Gordon Humble and I were posted to join 'D' Division; we had to report to Albany Street on 14 October 1957. However, something great was to happen before then. My sister Wendy and her fiancé David Hubbard were to be married on Saturday 12 October at Chipstead Parish Church. It was a topper and tails event; the ladies looked wonderful. And I was scolded by my mother for having a crew cut!

'Fancy coming to your sister's wedding and spoiling the photos. Can't you do something? Have it styled?'

5.

A memorable start

Two days later I reported with suitcase and suit-carrier to Albany Street Police Station, 'D' Division. It was rather daunting but exciting at the same time, although rather dampened by a rather unenthusiastic welcome from the Superintendent who said, 'This is an unusual step I'm taking – you are all going to St John's Wood, an old man's station. Get stuck in but don't try to make a name for yourselves.' We were introduced to Chief Superintendent Rogers – in those days that was the rank of the Divisional Commander – and he was warm, friendly and encouraging. Then we were given our divisional numbers – 367D – then John, Gordon and I were taken by police van to 199 Arlington Road, Camden Town – our section house for single men, almost opposite Railton House for down-and-outs.

Next day was our first as serving police officers, parading at 5.45 a.m., wondering what would be in store. How did I feel? Nervous, apprehensive, shy . . . but it turned out to be an incredible day. Paraded by Sergeant Rees, everyone except us three probationers were called by their Christian names; we were called by our new numbers. I was put with 'Brush' Broomhead, an older PC, to learn beats – for two weeks, as probationers had to do in those days – and we left the station after a cup of tea at about 6.20 a.m. Only another raw police officer will understand the mixed feelings that day – of pride, achievement, looking at one's reflection in shop windows; hoping that perhaps something might happen but nervous about the ability to cope.

There were few people about – milkmen, road sweepers, cleaners hurrying to work and so on; the newsagents' were open and gradually St John's Wood awoke. Traffic began to build up, shops opened, buses filled, the night-watchmen packed up and went home. Brush introduced me to this person and that; to shopkeepers in the High Street, to postmen, to cab drivers, to Sir Paul Bennett the senior magistrate as he strutted to the Tube to get to Marlborough Street Magistrates' Court, and to numerous others.

In those days, we had no radio – our means of communication was to visit a police box or post on our beat and 'ring in' on the direct line to the station; if the station wanted the constable on the beat, it could cause the box or post to flash its light; but bear in mind there were probably only two of these somewhere on a beat which may have been an area of five square miles! We carried a truncheon in a special long pocket inside the trouser leg and had a whistle plus key for the police box. Apart from various notebooks, that was our equipment.

So here I was, my first day in my new 'calling'. I was convinced that this was the right job for me, a young Christian with a lot to learn. I felt it was a true Christian commitment and while throughout my career I regularly asked God if he wanted me to serve him in any other capacity, I was anxious that as a follower of Christ, I would never be ashamed or shy about my faith amongst colleagues and senior officers; also, that on duty, there might be real opportunities to speak about Christ whenever it was right. I was to learn that there were times to keep my mouth shut – I was a police officer first of all. Yes, there were doubts and I am sure there were times when I should have spoken up and shied away from unseemly conversations. I knew then, and more so now, that I am nowhere near perfect, that I don't have all the answers and never did and that my attitude did not always reflect that of Christ.

Nevertheless, he had opened the way into the Metropolitan Police and here I was to prevent crime or do all I could to catch offenders if crime was committed. I was asked so many times either 'Can a Christian be a police officer?' or 'Can a police officer be a Christian?' The answer, I found, is 'Yes, of course.'

Already, I had inherited the nickname of my predecessor who had 367 as his number. He was an ardent Roman Catholic and, I suppose, word had got round that I was a 'churchie' so I was 'the Pope'. Even Brush had cottoned on to that but he was interested to know why I got the name since he was actually a Roman Catholic and all he got was 'Brush'! Nevertheless, it gave me an early opportunity to say that I was not 'religious' but was certainly a Christ follower. He listened well as we walked around the beat on that first and fascinating day. Yes, I felt very conspicuous!

Then we went in for breakfast at about 10.15 a.m. The canteen consisted of five tables, a two-ring gas cooker and a sink with a draining board. A rather brash cook came in at about 11 a.m. to start cooking lunch for the nine-to-fivers and I could see she was weighing me up when she arrived.

Then we were out on the streets again. We were asked questions, we helped people cross the road, we smiled – Brush certainly wasn't looking for trouble. In fact, at about 1.15 p.m., as we stood at the traffic lights of Circus Road and Wellington Road, he said, quietly, 'A nice little damage-only would suit us now. Exchange names and addresses then go in early to write it up.'

Suddenly there was a disturbance and urgent shouting further along Circus Road – 'He's gone down there! Stop, thief!' Someone ran up to us and said that a young man had snatched money from the underground station and had run off down the High Street.

'What's he look like?' Brush asked, apparently unconcerned.

'He's thin, in a brown jacket . . .'

Brush looked at me. 'Go on, Robin; get after him. If he continues running he might get back this way.'

So off I ran . . . I was fairly fit, still playing rugby and had only two weeks before come third in the Metropolitan Police 880 yards. So I hared off, holding my helmet under my arm, and saw this brown jacket at the bottom of the High Street. He turned right to go past the cabbies shelter and I lost sight of him but kept running.

As I passed the shelter, a taxi driver said, 'He's gone back up the main road!' But as I turned the corner, I saw, maybe a hundred yards ahead, the brown jacket jump through a hedge by the estate agents'. My heart was pounding but I went through the same hedge and saw this whimpering, brown-jacketed young man in a corner.

It wasn't long before several other people turned up to watch the arrest.

'That's him.'

'He deserves all he'll get!'

'Give him a hard time, copper.'

As I tried to catch my breath, I was thinking back to lesson sixty-seven, 'Arrests' and what to say! I could hear the sergeant saying, 'Even if you can't remember the exact words, you must give a caution that he needn't say anything . . .' This was daunting, my first real arrest. With all the noise and excitement, and Brush nowhere to be seen, I think I said something like, 'Have you stolen money from the Tube station?'

He nodded.

'I am arresting you for theft but don't say any more . . . yet.'

As I caught hold of him, he was as nervous as me and the crowd that followed us to the police station didn't help. Neither did Sergeant Rees who was about to book off duty.

'What a time to start arresting people, 367!'

Training school didn't prepare me for all the detail that had to go on just to get a prisoner charged and ready for court. But I quickly learnt – and from none other than Detective Sergeant 'Nipper' Read who happened to be in the station when the prisoner came in.

Actually, it seemed strange that I, in my size fourteen boots, in full uniform, caught up with and arrested this man. Listen! He was an Olympic athlete, having competed for Great Britain in Melbourne in 1956 – and I caught him on the run. Then I discovered that he wasn't a runner at all – he was a walker! Sadly, he was now hooked on drugs which he had originally taken as painkillers to cover an injury problem. Following the court case, in which he pleaded guilty, I spoke with him about faith in Christ, healing from him and a new life ahead. I knew I had to be careful when and where I said that but I felt that as he went to prison, he should at least know of God's love.

The next thirteen days of my 'puppy walking', or learning beats, didn't have the same excitement but I began to settle to the routine of early turn – up at 4.45

a.m. to parade three miles away at 5.45 a.m. and finish, hopefully, at 2 p.m.; then late turn, parade at 1.45 p.m. and off duty at 10 p.m. After those two weeks, it was out on our own and immediately on night duty parading at 9.45 p.m. and off duty next day at 6 a.m.

My first night out taught me a big lesson. Soon after 10 o'clock, I was walking at the statutory two-and-a-half miles an hour towards Maida Vale. I heard someone taking fast steps behind.

'Officer, please stop; I must speak to you.' I turned to see in the dim light of the street lamps, a rotund man, middle-aged, and highly agitated. 'Officer, do you know anything about the law?'

I responded with all the pride I could muster. Stretching myself to my full six foot five inches, thumbs in my jacket chest pockets, I said, 'Sir, I am the law!'

'Well, in that case, help me.' He then rattled out all the problems of his marital life!

Then came the court case from my first arrest. In the senior stage at Peel House, we had had two sessions of giving evidence, and had even been cross-questioned by instructors posing as lawyers, but it wasn't the same as the real thing. As I stood in the foyer of Marylebone Magistrates' Court, a real fear came over me. I prayed but the nerves were still there. Within a couple of minutes, I was called into the witness box and was led through my evidence. Then the magistrate, in front of whom I stood many times after that, simply said, 'Good job you were fit, officer; well done.'

I never ever got over the nerves which I experienced during my first case; whenever I had to give evidence, I had 'butterflies' – but at least it encouraged me to pray hard before going into court!

6.

Life in St John's Wood

As a rookie, one is rather nervous of the 'stars' of this life, many of whom lived in St John's Wood or Hampstead.

One day, I was called by some pedestrians to the top of St John's Wood High Street where there was a zebra crossing. A rather plush car was badly parked and a motor scooter rider had fallen off trying to avoid a child on the crossing.

The rider was apparently unhurt and had ridden away before I arrived; the child had been pulled away by his nanny and was nowhere to be seen; but the car was still in a dangerous position and it was obvious that something had to be done. I pulled out my notebook but before I wrote anything down a rather large man came out of a shop and called out, "'allo, 'allo! What 'ave we 'ere?'

It was Tommy Trinder – a very well-known comedian – but I didn't recognise him.

'Sir,' I said, 'is this your car?'

'Yes, nice one isn't it?'

'Please move it. I'd like to speak to you.'

'You can speak to me here, officer!' By now, he was playing to the gathering audience. 'He called me "sir"! Thank you, officer. No one's ever given me a title!'

A Traffic Patrol colleague on his motorcycle drew up; sensing a problem, he got off and said to me, 'Having difficulties?'

'Yes, this man won't move his car and it's already caused an accident.'

'Leave it with me.' My colleague, Stan Hyde, spoke to Mr Trinder. 'Are you the driver of this car?'

'I was,' he replied, laughing.

'Then move it now, please, to the other side of the crossing.' It was said with such authority and confidence that Tommy Trinder did as he was asked. But he was soon up to his tricks again singing the song 'The Laughing Policeman'. The crowd loved it and applauded him.

Some weeks later, I was in Marylebone Magistrates' Court for Tommy Trinder's appearance. Tommy Trinder's lawyer asked me a few questions but there was no dispute or any laughter. Tommy was very subdued. Eventually the case concluded with Tommy apologising to the court and to Stan and me; he was given a conditional discharge.

But many of the celebrities I met in the course of my duties were a delight; they were generous to us as police officers, giving to charities, signing autographs which we could pass on to disadvantaged children that we knew . . . One celebrity I often met was Norman Wisdom. He became a good friend even then and later, on the Isle of Man.

My first duty involving any member of the royal family was when I had less than a year's service. A sergeant and three constables were deployed to Park Road where Her Majesty the Queen Mother had been invited to open a renovated building which would house one of her favourite charities, of which she was patron. At the station, we were inspected as to the smartness of our uniform and expected to gently ensure a safe and uninterrupted passage for Her Majesty across the forecourt away from, and then back to, her car.

A number of people had arrived to catch a glimpse of Her Majesty and, of course, those working within the building were lined up outside.

I was in awe as Her Majesty arrived to polite but enthusiastic applause; her beaming smile never changed as she was welcomed and introduced to various people. She said a few encouraging words and cut the tape before disappearing inside. An hour or so later, she reappeared and said her farewells. She didn't immediately go to her car but approached our sergeant, thanked him for being there on duty and asked to be introduced to the three constables. She simply shook our hands gently and said to us all, 'Thank you so much for taking time from your busy lives.'

It was through the Christian life of Queen Elizabeth the Queen Mother, I believe, that I began to think through the notion that it was the way I lived, the way I talked to people, the way of compassion and listening, of accepting people as they were – even those in trouble who I met as a police officer – which could influence people towards belief in Christ. We never know what part we play in someone else's path to faith; if we are honest it can backfire when our life is not matching up to what we believe – that we don't actually walk the talk.

My years at St John's Wood were spent in great company. I soon learned that it was quite profitable to have a bicycle and become an 'authorised cyclist' for three weeks at a time. Phillip Williams and I were the cyclists one night. We did that for which we were trained on our respective patrols for an hour or so and then met up with the intention of going down to the Edgware Road where the action was. En route we stopped at a pie stall opposite Marylebone Railway Station, which was in a different sub-division. There we were, leaning on our bikes, slightly off our 'ground' surreptitiously eating our pies when two men shouted for us from across the road because a man was breaking into a flat.

What happened to the half-eaten pies I don't know but the men pointed to some flats down the road, in York Street, and said that the man had broken a window and climbed in. By the time we had searched for and found the broken window, there was a man climbing out. Phill and I nabbed him. I knew what to say by then and, as we searched him, we realised that we had a genuine burglar. The only trouble was that we were in the wrong place and had to take the prisoner to Marylebone Lane Police Station. No one seemed to query how it was that we, from St John's Wood, had nabbed a burglar near Gloucester Place.

Another bonus in having a bike was to spend much of my time when off duty riding through the streets of London. My endeavour was to get to know the Metropolitan area as well as possible with its streets and landmarks because a police officer was nearly always the first person a stranger would ask for directions. The potential black taxi cab drivers in London have to learn over 400 different routes and I often saw them – usually on a moped – with a board fixed precariously in front of them, learning their way around the capital. I was doing a similar thing except that I would get out my A–Z, pick a point some ten miles away, and trace a route to reach it, coming back a different way. Of course, having worked in Horseferry Road, I already knew many of the central streets and buildings.

I soon was given a place in the divisional rugby team. We played other divisions and civilian teams; we had some real scraps, the only drawback being that our home ground was at Hendon, many miles away. Not long after I joined the force, I began to see more of Chris as she was nursing at St Thomas's; on her off-duty days, when she could, she would come to the rugby matches and to various police functions.

I was thoroughly enjoying the camaraderie and the challenges of policing. But there were some unpleasant incidents. Once, I witnessed a horrendous traffic accident when a private car sped across a junction in Abbey Road and rammed a heavy lorry. The lorry dragged the car which was under the chassis at least twenty yards and the sparks ignited the leaking petrol from the crushed car. I could see the driver of the car still inside and I dived under the lorry, somehow managing to get the unconscious and burning man out of the car's broken window and drag him away from the fire. At least I got a new uniform in exchange for my burnt and irreparable one!

There were also some near-disasters, such as the night when I was in the canteen eating my sandwiches at about 2.30 a.m. when 113 Smith came puffing upstairs very agitated. An intruder had been seen climbing on to the roof of a local radio factory. Phill and I dashed out, putting on our jackets and helmets as we ran to the roundabout at Wellington Road. We raced across to the factory in Lodge Road – the gates were swinging open. We stopped in the shadows and heard the sound of breaking glass somewhere above us.

'Wait here,' I told Phill. 'I'll go up and flush him out. He's bound to come out this way, so grab him.'

With some difficulty and scraping of boots, I shinned up a drainpipe, over the gutter and on to the roof. It would have been a real giveaway to use my torch. So it was dark as I crept along the sloping roof. Then I glimpsed movement ahead; I lost sight of him, but in taking one more step, my foot went through the hole in the broken window and stopped me dead. Had I taken just one more step, I would have gone over the end of the building and down a ventilator shaft to the underground railway below.

It was a close shave but there was no time to mop up the blood from what felt like (and actually was) a gaping wound through the tear in my trousers. I wanted that prisoner. Somehow, I eased my way back to the drainpipe and, feeling my way very gingerly, I heard a scuffle below. Phill had pinned the prisoner to the ground. Breaking and entering, factory breaking, assault on police . . . some time later, he went down for three years.

I was the radio operator on Delta 3, our area car; Dusty Miller was the driver – he later drove with the Flying Squad out of Scotland Yard. We heard a call to an abattoir in Paddington where thieves were on the premises. No other car answered the call and, after a nod from Dusty, I acknowledged the call: 'On way!' We drove at high speed through the night, with me trying to find the street from the map with a wobbling and swaying torch. We screeched to a halt and I was first out to try and discover if there was a break-in.

I could hear sounds which seemed to come from the roof. There was a ladder attached to the end wall of the building, absolutely vertical.

'I'm going up,' I whispered to Dusty.

I was soon on the sloping tiles. There ahead of me, silhouetted against the skyline of early dawn, was a man running up the tiles and over the ridge. I had just reached the peak when my footing went and I slipped backwards, accelerating fast. Scrabbling for some hold, I knew I had lost it but one of my feet caught in the gutter and slewed me round to the point that I was lying sideways, grimly holding on to the gutter with my bleeding left hand. Hoping it wouldn't give way, I somehow released my twisted foot and looked down at sixty feet of nothingness except the blood and gore inside the abattoir.

Obviously, I survived – but we lost a prisoner or two. Dusty got us to Paddington Green Police Station, not only to report what had happened but also to get a large mug of tea for a shaken young man. At least I didn't lose my head for heights! Sitting in the canteen back at St John's Wood, I had to laugh when a colleague who knew the abattoir called out, 'I wonder what an Oake sausage would have tasted like?'

As I walked along Lodge Road and the long road-bridge over a number of railway lines going to and from Marylebone Station, and underground lines alongside, my thoughts were disturbed by just one shriek from below: 'It's coming.' Only a man of six foot five could see over the brick wall. I spotted three youths scampering across the lines, then ducking behind one of the bridge pillars. There had been trouble with kids before on these lines. The only way down was to go along to the junction with Park Road; the gate with steps behind it was usually unlocked. I ran for the gate, and climbed down the rusty rungs of steps, and dashed across the electric lines of the underground, which was above ground there. Then I heard the ear-piercing screech of brakes, wheels screaming as they skidded on metal, and a huge bang – I saw the steam engine off the rails and on its side, smoke belching from and engulfing the engine; it had pulled and twisted one carriage with it, although the carriage didn't topple. The rest of the train was upright. I was only maybe twenty yards from this scene and saw between the coal-tender and that first carriage the youths running across other lines away from me. I recognised the last of the three but they were soon out of sight and my first concern was the driver and fireman in the engine.

There was so much steam and smoke and scattered coal, but as I leaped across the lines, the driver and his mate appeared at the top (which was really the side) of the toppled engine. Apart from a few bruises, they were OK – but furious. They had seen the two sleepers jammed in the rails but it was too late to do anything as they came out from the bridge – which was, in fact, like a short tunnel, and dark. No passengers were injured. Miraculously, people appeared – two fire engines, at least two ambulances, railway police . . . I didn't hang around for long. I knew one of the lads and I knew where he lived. I soon found him.

Back at the station, there was a complaint from a passer-by that I had derailed the train! The one boy that I had recognised was a smart lad and despite all our efforts, he confessed to nothing, wouldn't say who his friends were – and then I realised that I hadn't actually seen him put the sleepers on the line. Circumstantial evidence, however obvious, can be inaccurate. He eventually agreed that he was on the tracks that day and was cautioned for trespassing. That's justice!

One late turn, and just after parading, Sergeant Rees took me by the elbow and said, 'Robin, what are you like with suicides? I've got an unusual one for you.' He told me the location, a local block of flats, and told me to go to the sixth floor and meet the nanny there. Not knowing any other detail, I went.

The nanny came to the door, very distressed. She invited me in and, sobbing almost uncontrollably, told me that the pet poodle had jumped through the open rear window of a bedroom and was lying dead in the basement area below. Sure enough, I looked out and there was the white poodle, apparently lifeless, in a pool of blood. Suicide? Did the nanny throw it out? Was it an accident? I hurriedly took all the details I could, asked the nanny to telephone the police station for a vet and went down to see if the dog was actually dead. The vet eventually arrived, pronounced death and, looking at the tiny bitch, said, 'Did she leave a note?'

I tried to stifle a laugh.

'No, no,' the vet said, 'sorry! I meant, did the owner leave a fiver for me?'

But on the subject of suicides, it is never a job that an officer likes. I was the radio operator with Chippy Carpenter as driver when Delta 3 was again sent off its ground to Paddington; the address given and the final word from the Information Room was, 'Woman lying injured – ambulance on way.'

We took some time to find the high-rise flats but we were the first to arrive. A small crowd had gathered.

Someone shouted, 'She's over here.'

Sure enough, there was the crumpled body of a middle-aged woman lying in a basement area. Enquiries told us that she had climbed over the balcony railings of her apartment and, after hesitation, had either jumped or fallen. We called for a police surgeon and after noting witness details, went up to the flat, met the caretaker. We let ourselves in through the front door and, in the lounge, saw the open sash window from which she had jumped. On the table of a very tidy and well-furnished room was a scribbled note:

> God has let me down. He has left me and now I can't stand living anymore.

There were no other clues as to what could have happened or anything untoward to indicate a crime, but I put together a very sad account of a lady who had lost her husband, was estranged from her grown-up children and had believed that she was seriously ill; she was awaiting a hospital examination. She was alone with apparently very few friends or visitors, and it seemed that the loneliness had driven her to a leap into eternity.

This was a turning point in my early career and, more so, in my young faith – I resolved to ensure that I kept vigilant, and had a perceptive ear for any in our station area who might be facing a similar situation.

7.

Sharing the faith

By meeting poverty, even in the midst of the wealth of north London, or coming across single-parent families, or families suffering at the hands of an alcoholic father or mother (or both) – indeed, any whose needs were not met by any form of policing – I found the opportunity to put into practice the practical side of my Christian faith. I would spend time listening, counselling when I could, putting people in touch with social services, the Citizens' Advice Bureau or even the Samaritans. This extra service, to me, was humbling but very satisfying.

Primrose Hill Park, opposite Regent's Park and London Zoo, was a busy place, especially at weekends. Children with their families played happily together on the grass and on the swings, the roundabout and in the sandpit. I was walking through the Park one Sunday afternoon when a nanny, with two young children, made an allegation against an unkempt man who was sitting on a bench. There had been some minor comments recently about leering men – either looking at children or the attractive nannies and young mums – but nothing more than that. So here was another complaint, very general: 'I don't like the look of him.' There was

insufficient evidence to make an arrest but my obvious
duty was to ask him to move.

So I spoke to the man, discovered his name and asked
him to move out of Primrose Hill. We walked together
and talked and, although in a dishevelled state and
probably having had too much to drink, I discovered
that he was formerly an accountant from the Home
Counties, had had family problems, had fallen on hard
times and was now living in a bedsit by himself.

I offered him a New Testament I was carrying, and
challenged him to read it. He willingly took it. Some
weeks later, while I was radio operator in Delta 3, I saw
the same man walking along the pavement in Regent's
Park Road and asked the driver, Ron Bishop, to do a
U-turn so that I could speak to him. As we drew alongside, I wound down the window. But before I could
speak, he thrust his head through the window and,
somehow, also his hand with the New Testament in it.
He said, very excitedly, 'One of your colleagues gave me
this book to read. I tell you I have read it and I have
changed! It's made a man of me.'

I used to see this man occasionally before he returned
home. He had clearly been 'born again'; the grace of God
had reached and healed him. I prayed often that his family would receive him back with enthusiasm.

Late one evening, I had a call to a family where there
had been an almighty argument, tempers lost, shouting
and throwing china and so on. The man of the house had
run away before I arrived on my bike so when I walked
in, I found a very distressed wife and three children, all
crying. There were no complaints or obvious injuries;
the dispute had been started by a minor disagreement
which escalated into irrational behaviour. I sat with the
family and even made a cup of tea; soon equilibrium

was restored and the two youngest children went to bed leaving the wife and her son, aged about fourteen. We chatted and laughed together and, suddenly, the husband let himself in. I thought, 'Here we go again.' But he went straight to his wife, simply said, 'I am so sorry; it was all my fault' and she burst into tears and mumbled something about forgiveness.

Some days later, I was in the area and popped in to see the family. The husband said how grateful he was that I had come. Then he said, 'There was something about you or your attitude that moved us so much. What is it you've got that we haven't?' Difficult to answer such a question! Still, I spoke about my weird sense of humour . . . and also about my Christian faith.

'Tell us about it; we don't go to church,' he said.

'It isn't about going to church or being religious,' I replied, and simply told them how I had become a Christian. Amazingly, both husband and wife asked if it was not too late for them to follow suit! They knew nothing then of the grace of God so I spent a few minutes explaining the way of salvation to them; how Jesus died on the cross to pay the penalty for all the wrong things we have done that have separated us from our holy God, and how, through him, we can have a new life. They both knelt with me in the lounge and prayed to receive Christ into their lives. How I cherished the friendship of that family while I was at St John's Wood, seeing them growing in faith and their children, too, as they settled into a lively local church.

I was jailer for a tour of duty at St John's Wood and I clearly remember speaking with a young man who had been arrested for drunkenness and was sobering up. Enquiries had shown this man, a carpenter by trade, had been in trouble through drink on numerous occasions.

Sober, he was an interesting man to talk with; he pleaded with me to do anything I could to get him off drink. I spoke about counselling, Alcoholics Anonymous and even psychiatric treatment until he said he had tried everything. He was in his cell, alone, no other prisoners, so I took the opportunity to talk about Jesus the healer. He listened, and his interest deepened when he heard of my faith. I told him that being a Christian was not having all troubles swept away but Jesus could heal, forgive and give new life. From the words of the Bible, I showed this sad man that Jesus had died for him and was now alive; that he would come into his life if he acknowledged his sin, and his illness. So there I was, with a needy man, now pleading for the Lord Jesus to come into his life.

Next day, I went to Court with him, although it wasn't my case; he expected a custodial sentence but the magistrate, incredibly with the long list of convictions, gave him a conditional discharge – the condition being that he sought help from the Salvation Army or Alcoholics Anonymous.

As we left court, the man said, 'That's my second prayer answered – I'm free.'

I said, 'What was your first prayer?'

'Asking Jesus into my life in the cell!'

Sundays were often days of opportunity in regard to sharing my faith, since many of our calls were to domestic disputes in homes. I suppose I was never really keen to work on a Sunday but ruefully accepted it as part of the 'fun' of policing! As I walked up St John's Wood High Street at about 9 o'clock, I was musing that I had another hour on duty and then a very short sleep to be back on duty at 5.45 a.m. next morning. Then a lady came out of a highly respectable hostelry, and accidentally bumped into me.

'Oops, sorry officer – ah, it's you, Robin. I've been to church and had my Guinness and all's right with the world.'

I knew this lady who was the manager at a local dry cleaning business. I walked with her along the street for some while; we talked about this and that, and eventually I asked her about her church. I soon found out that she didn't know about the grace of God and why Jesus had died for her – a conversation which didn't end that night. I occasionally popped into her place of work and inevitably came back to the subject of Christianity until the day came when she said she was not good enough to be a Christian.

'We all have to come just as we are,' I explained. 'Respectable people leading an upright life or alcoholics and thieves can all meet the Lord Jesus. He accepts us all just as we are.'

That afternoon, in the shop, she prayed to receive Christ, for him to forgive and make her new.

Another time, I went to assist an elderly but very articulate lady who was struggling with her shopping as she walked past Lord's Cricket Ground. I was on duty, in uniform, and as I walked along carrying the bags in one hand, with her clinging to my other arm, we had quite a conversation. She asked what I did at weekends and I told her about my sport and church.

'Are you an active Christian?' I asked.

'That's a bit cheeky,' she said. 'There's no need to worry about me – my nephew is a bishop!'

Sadly, our connections – however good they are – will not be the passport to eternal life.

One sad side of policing is coming to terms with sudden death and, more difficult, informing relatives about it. My Christian faith was a tremendous help in a very practical way, for if I was given a 'death' message to take the bad news, I could pray for wisdom – what to say, when to shut up, how to listen, whether to seek a neighbour or other relative if the person was alone, arranging transport to the hospital or mortuary and so on. I never got used to it but have, wonderfully, made many good friends through such tragedies. I also had the reputation of being 'right' for this and probably dealt with such messages more than most of my colleagues. Although I had to take some stick for being an active Christian, I felt privileged to be asked to deal with these instances.

Some of the awful deaths were in road traffic accidents but perhaps the most horrific was in Northgate – a large old-style apartment block in Prince Albert Road where many well-known celebrities lived. This particular day, I was walking my beat and saw a fire engine parked outside one of the entrances, its blue lights still flashing. The driver was standing by the engine speaking into a microphone but hailed me.

'You're needed on the sixth floor but the lift isn't working. There's been an accident.'

I hurriedly climbed the stairs and was breathing heavily when I arrived. Firemen were there and a porter. A headless body was impaled on the lift guard railings. A bloody mess, literally.

What had happened, I gradually discovered, was that the concierge was on a ladder leaning over the railings cleaning the inside of the cage when the lift came down from above and struck him. What a disaster . . . for the man, his family and, indeed for the person riding in the lift and the porter.

Having done what had to be done, firstly using a telephone in one of the flats to tell the sergeant and call the CID just in case there was anything suspicious about the incident, I returned to the station and was given the task of going to speak to the dead man's wife. My prayer was answered in a remarkable way; she was at home – it being about 2.30 p.m. – and her daughter was visiting her. As soon as they saw my uniform they knew there was bad news. I broke it to them about there being an accident without going into any detail, and that the husband and father had died instantly. Of course there were tears. Then the wife said to me, 'We're Christians. We'll find this hard but our faith will carry us through.' This gave me the opportunity to pray with them both, to visit them again, attend the inquest with them and go to the funeral at their active and caring church. I had found some lovely friends.

Once, I was walking towards Finchley Road in Ordnance Hill, when a man, complete with bowler hat, dark overcoat and briefcase, suddenly fell some yards in front of me. As I approached him, I wondered why he wasn't trying to get up. When I knelt beside him, I could see his blue lips; I felt for a pulse – none – and turned him on his back to try the old method of artificial respiration which we had been taught in training school. No response. I had shouted to the small crowd of commuters and shoppers on their way to the Tube station, and asked someone to phone for an ambulance. Eventually, an ambulance arrived but my efforts to revive the well-dressed man failed.

I doubted that the ambulance would take a dead body. However, presumably it being the most expedient thing to do and out of sympathy for me, they put the body on a stretcher and into the back of the ambulance and I accompanied them to St John and St Elizabeth Hospital. The attendant did try more heart massage but still no response. When we arrived at the hospital, a doctor came into the ambulance and pronounced the man dead.

As I stepped down I was met by an ultra-efficient Sister.

'What religion is he?' she demanded.

How on earth would I know? I had only just met the man – and he was dead when I met him! I then discovered, having been given a lecture, that there were three mortuaries – one for Jews, one for Roman Catholics and one for Others. The Sister decided he was an 'Other'!

This incident bothered me for some time. Why was there such demarcation? I recognised that there would be different rights to perform and therefore the rabbi, the priest or any other denominational minister would care for a particular dignity but my concern was regarding reaching the gates of heaven. Did God ask the same question – 'Which religion are you?' No; I believed his ultimate question will be something like, 'What did you think of or do with my Son, Jesus Christ?'

In policing, every day is different. Between 7.45 a.m. and 9.30 a.m., there were several places in London where police assisted rush hour traffic at particularly busy junctions, mainly to cut off what we called the 'tail-enders' who persistently tried to beat the system by continuing into a junction on the amber light, causing a tailback.

I was at the Prince Albert Road junction with Avenue Road – very busy east-west and north-south traffic. At about 8.25 a.m., a black saloon crept past me as I stood there with my white gauntlets; the rear window of the car was down and a cheery voice called out 'You're doing a good job, Robin.' It was Chief Superintendent Rogers, the boss.

Sometime after 8.30 a.m., when the traffic was at its heaviest, a car stalled as the green light came up and the male driver failed to get it started, so missed a phase of the lights. That caused a cacophony of car horns behind him while he tried again and again to start the engine. The build-up was quickly bad tempered with shouting and, after another phase had passed, I saw two men, wearing overalls, walking along the pavement. I called to them to help me push the car across the junction.

With a few grins – 'What me, help the law?' – they assisted me; the driver was very relieved to be moving, albeit without an engine. As I pushed from the side, the workmen at the rear of the car, it suddenly lost it slow momentum; I looked over my shoulder to see one of the men lying face down in the road, with his mate trying to lift him.

I thought he had just tripped, but his mate said, 'I think he's dead.'

I bent down and sure enough, no breathing, no pulse.

'Get an ambulance, quick!' I shouted. I struggled to turn the dead man over and give him the breath of life. There was now an orchestra and choir of blasting horns and shouting from the windows of cars. I was conscious of chaos as vehicles on the inside lane tried to get out to the crowded outside lane.

My efforts – breathing into a dead mouth, thumping and pumping an unresponsive chest – had exhausted me. Onlookers seemed to be pinned to the spot. I shouted for some of them to push the car away on to the pavement. But of course, I shouldn't have done that for I was then in danger because I was below the eye-line in the road with a dead man.

The ambulance eventually came weaving its way through rush hour traffic; the attendants took the dead workman away. I went across to his friend; he was on his haunches, leaning against a wall, in tears, deeply shaken. I gradually got some details and told him where the body was. I admit I was tempted to ask that rueful question 'What religion is he?' but no doubt the Sister had sorted that out.

That wasn't the end. Having discovered his full details at the hospital from the wallet he had in his pocket, the family had to be informed – not by me this time as he lived some distance away. I met his wife later at the coroner's inquest. That was an ordeal – not so much giving my evidence, but facing the family, since I was the one who could be accused of causing the death. Incredibly, the dead man's wife, with her children, came to me in the foyer of the court and expressed deep sympathy for me. I tried to apologise, recognising that I could be blamed. Her words have remained with me: 'You are forgiven; no blame on you.'

8.

Chris

At this time, I was still seeing Chris. She was a nurse at St Thomas's Hospital, opposite the Houses of Parliament so we weren't that far away from each other; we courted at quite unusual times of the day and into the night simply because our shift duties were difficult to match.

When we couldn't see each other, she often listened to the police frequency on the radio and heard the various calls to cars on duty. One particular night, she heard a call go to Delta 3 which simply gave the location – and reason: 'St John's Wood High Street, junction with Circus Road – PC 367 needs urgent assistance.' I had disturbed a shop-breaker who leaped a wall behind the shops and into very dark bushes. I needed some assistance because I was sure I had him cornered and had been to get a taxi driver to radio for assistance.

Within minutes – which seemed much longer – Delta 3 arrived and although members of the crew had much more service than me, I was in the unenviable position of telling them what I wanted and where I wanted them. My first leadership role!

It was pitch black. My comrades let the suspect know that they were police officers; the man immediately broke cover, still carrying a heavy sack of 'swag'. I chased after him and literally felt his collar about eighty yards further on. 'You're nicked! Don't say anything.' Then, back at the station, I properly cautioned the prisoner.

All this time, Chris had been listening to the radio, anxious to hear what had happened. I believe she was very relieved to hear: 'Delta 3. Reference your message at 23.56, "PC needs urgent assistance"; one prisoner with 367 to Delta Sierra.'

Some days later, when I was on night duty as radio operator, I took up the handset and gave our position to the Information Room who asked me to keep a commentary going about an incident. Chris, in the nurses' home, had again been listening to the radio on the police waveband. She had dozed off but heard my voice. Startled, she thought I had come to see her. But she was entertained as we followed a stolen lorry through the streets of north London, and eventually arrested the driver.

One of the odd duties of a constable is to deal with lost and found property. Perhaps the strangest thing that happened regarding property during my days on the beat was when one day, very early in the morning, as I walked along King Henry's Road, I saw a skull tucked under a hedge. I knelt down and wondered where the rest of the body was. There was no sign of any other bones in the vicinity so I picked up the skull and examined it. No clues as to its identity, its gender or its age; it was clean so there was no chance that someone had lost their head overnight. I tucked it under my arm and began the walk back to the station – which was some way from where I found the skull.

I began to smile to myself. I made my way via Elsworthy Road, Queen's Grove and then the High

Street, where I knew the skull would cause a few comic remarks.

The butcher happened to be putting up his shop blind as I walked past.

'You eaten all the meat?'

Someone else made a comment about Yorik in *Hamlet*; another wanted to know where its hair had gone and someone else asked, 'Have you lost a body?'

The strange look I had from Sergeant Tooze was the best thing, however. A meticulous man in every detail, he stared hard while I said, 'Sarge, I've found part of a body.'

'Well,' he said, at length, 'where's the rest of it?'

I thought he was going to order me back to the hedge for a search!

'Sarge, this is clean and probably stolen from either a collection or most probably from the biology department at a local school. If you like, I'll ring round and let you know the result.'

Sure enough, the second school I contacted rang me back to say that the skull of their skeleton had gone missing and was probably taken by a pupil. It was taken back by car.

Once, Phill and I were waiting for deck-chair thieves – property had gone missing from a grassed area at the centre of the graveyard at St John's Wood Church. We waited for three nights – no thieves. Still, the children's playground was also there and we amused ourselves on the swings and roundabout. But the slides proved a problem. I climbed the ladder and gingerly sat at the top of the slide but became firmly wedged about three feet down. With my bulky raincoat and added width from my truncheon, the more I tried to move, the worse it got. Phill did eventually get me down by pushing, levering, and then dragging my feet. It created quite a hole in my right thigh. Then we patrolled through the gravestones and began to read the inscriptions. Some were fascinating and we asked unanswered questions, allowing our imaginations to wonder about the circumstances of death. We found a tomb structure like a large square coffin – but made of stone. It had a large crack through which we attempted to see inside with our torches. Phill, in trying to widen the crack a little, brought the whole stone slab down – on my right foot! It took both of us to move it just a little so that I could escape. After hobbling to the station and booking off, Phill drove me to St Thomas's Hospital casualty department. I received treatment to the broken toe and the hole in my thigh from the earlier incident on the slide.

Chris arrived. Word had reached her from a colleague that I was in casualty and she had imagined that I was badly hurt. Instead, I was laughing my way through the treatment – although I did feel rather embarrassed.

However, the following day I began to be ill, swelling up; rather than be detained in a section house, I was able to get transport home to my parents, who hardly recognised me. I went straight to bed, and the doctor was called.

'Not rugby again, Robin?' he said.

I mumbled something about the gravestone and hospital.

He finished the sentence ' . . . and you had an anti-tetanus injection.'

'Yes.'

I was suffering from an overdose, having had too much of the serum from previous rugby injuries. I had lockjaw.

I didn't return to duty for six weeks and then I was on light duties for a month.

As an active member of the Christian Police Association, I was frequently invited to join teams of three or four colleagues to take services in churches in and around London. Then, on occasions, we would go away for a weekend. It was when returning from one of these trips that I was taken ill with what seemed to be stomach cramps. Again I was admitted to St Thomas's Hospital where appendicitis was diagnosed. Within an hour I was in the operating theatre and woke up next morning with a nurse in full uniform leaning over me and whispering sweet nothings . . . I thought I knew that voice . . . through the blur of anaesthesia and soreness, I realised that yes, it was Chris.

When I was discharged from hospital, I went to the Police Convalescent Home at Hove, Sussex. And here I prayed something specific – that if Chris came to visit me, I would propose to her. Sure enough, my parents were able to pick her up during her days off and bring her down by car; I seem to remember that we went along the front to Brighton, had tea for four and toast for eight; yes, my appetite was coming back and I needed strength. My parents sussed that something was up and went for a stroll while Chris and I went to the beach. I was more nervous about this than about giving evidence in court and although I had planned what I wanted to say, it didn't seem to come out right. With a thumping heart and dry mouth, I blurted out what could not have been a very elegant proposal of marriage but, incredibly, without even a hint of delay or consideration, Chris accepted my proposal. We were over the moon, as they say, but we didn't announce it – not then! I knew I would have to speak seriously with her father before we could officially be engaged. We 22-year-olds blew a sigh of relief when both her mother and father formally approved of our engagement.

The next item was the ring. Oh dear – a nurse on a pittance and a police constable on little more. Some months before, I had saved some money and had a loan from my dad so that I could purchase a 1934 Austin 10; I was so proud of it, and it was also the most useful item of any worth that I possessed. It was the car or a ring.

After much heart-searching, I put the car up for sale and, with the proceeds, bought a stone for Chris' left hand.

'Back at the ranch' I was given experience in the CID under Detective Sergeant 'Nipper' Read which was exhilarating and challenging. As a young aide, there was little serious investigation, collating evidence or court work but one's prowess was seen by initiatives that were taken. One of my colleagues (usually very smartly dressed, with a white, stiff collar and old school tie), dressed in old and smelly ragged clothes, adopted a hobble with hunched shoulders, and booked into Rowton House, the hostel in Arlington Road, Camden Town to sleep with the down-and-outs for one shilling (5p) a night. An unpleasant way of listening to who was where and what they were doing, to be sure, but he got some excellent information and arrests!

I thoroughly enjoyed the experience with the CID but it did not lead on to a career in that department. My old friend, Ron Perrett, drew my attention to a notice in the twice-weekly *Police Orders* which were published to indicate personnel matters and to advertise vacancies within the force, plus changes in law and/or procedure. The notice was seeking applications for a post in 'A' Department, New Scotland Yard. It sounded like an opportunity for a change in experience, so I prayed this through and sent in my CV. I had already learnt that if I pushed the door, I could trust

God either to keep it shut or to open it and I'd be happy with either decision.

Some weeks later, I was given a time for interview in 'A' Department and was daunted to be entering the halls of New Scotland Yard for the very first time. I was asked how my Christian faith could work as a police officer; this was the second time I had been asked that question, the first being at my initial interview to join the police. My reply must have been acceptable as I was successful. And in January 1961 I began a new aspect of policing which was to stand me in good stead for the rest of my career.

My last Christmas on the beat – I volunteered to be on duty since most of my colleagues were married with families and I was single – meant parading with just two other constables at 5.45 a.m. and no visit from Santa Claus! It was great to see the Christmas lights, watching bedroom lights coming on very early, hearing the screeches of young children as they opened their stockings.

Then at about 7.30 a.m. I was crossing Finchley Road into Circus Road when I heard a different sort of screeching – the screech of brakes, of skidding, of one collision, then another and a third . . . and silence. I ran towards the noise and as I rounded the bend, saw a car on its roof, a lot of debris in the road behind it – and nobody about. It was eerie. I went down on my haunches to see if I could help the driver (and, of course, there were no seat-belts then) who was upside down and, surprisingly, only slightly hurt. I helped him out, asked if he wanted to go to hospital or see a doctor but he declined.

There was still nobody around; I had no way of contacting the station. Apart from the car on its roof, three others were quite severely damaged. The driver couldn't account for his accident – I thought he had nodded off –

but I did what I had been taught at training school, though never had needed or dared to do before. Remember, there was no one about so, almost as a joke, I shouted at the top of my voice: 'Did anyone see what happened?' I really *was* joking – and it was Christmas.

To my surprise, a lady's voice came as if from heaven: 'Yes, I did!'

I looked up. On the top floor of a high block of flats in Circus Road, a woman was leaning out of her open sash window.

'Stay where you are,' I said. 'I'll be up in a few minutes!'

Only two weeks later, I was being greeted by Chief Superintendent Bill Best in 'A' Department, CO. He was very welcoming and helped me to relax but immediately taught me how to copy his signature to make it look authentic, which after several amateurish attempts, I managed to do. Then, he showed me how to open and re-seal an envelope without leaving a clue that it had been touched! It was done for a good and sound reason but seemed a little odd as my first exercise as Oake of the Yard.

The work was highly specialised. Suffice to say, it was also a highly competitive job and accuracy was a key element. It was demanded that we all sat promotion examinations at the earliest opportunity.

Soon after I had entered this new phase of my life, Chris and I were married in Purley Baptist Church – 1st April 1961, Easter Saturday. A number of old and new colleagues came to the service and reception along with many of Chris' nursing friends. I had asked Ron Perrett to be my best man – he did it superbly. I also asked Phill Williams, by now in the Traffic Department, to be our getaway driver so that everyone expecting to shower us with foam, rice and sticky confetti, and looking to tying balloons and kippers to the car, would be foiled. No one guessed it was Phill's car parked at the exit of the church car park.

Chris and I had a wonderful honeymoon in Guernsey and then returned to our small flat in West Croydon, and continued to work in London. We soon moved to another apartment, this time in Battersea. We were on the fifth floor and there was no lift; when our son, Stephen Robin was born – after quite a difficult pregnancy and birth – on 21 April 1962, it was a hassle to get shopping, baby and, at first, a pram and a bicycle up seventy-six stairs. We eventually persuaded the caretaker to open up a large cupboard on the ground floor that the pram and my bike could fit in.

Studying at home for my promotion exam at this time was not easy. Chris bore my long visits to the local library with a cheerful acceptance. The day of the exam came – a Saturday – and I went to Peel House to work through the three-hour paper. When the ordeal was over, I came out and, to my surprise, there was Chris with Steve in the pram, waiting! She had been watching me through a window. Weeks later, I had the great news that I had passed.

Working in CO opened my eyes to new aspects of policing and its many departments; it also introduced me to a new kind of social life. For the first time ever, I was encouraged to buy a dinner suit since most evening functions we attended meant wearing formal dress. But what happy years I had, in a tightly knit group, all working together, each with great humour and dedication! Yes, so far, Gilbert was wrong.

9.

In greater hands

It was snowing heavily in January 1963 when Chris, Steve (now nine months old) and I were staying in Coulsdon, Surrey with my parents-in-law. We hadn't intended to stay so long after Christmas but the winter weather at that time was both magnificent and treacherous. I had to report to Superintendent Colin Woods at West End Central on the first Monday in January in full uniform (the stripes has been proudly sewn on by Chris) with the new number (40 'C', and with my height the new nickname – Forty Towers). I went by train on its reduced service knowing that the formalities would be over soon after lunch so that I could go back to Coulsdon, pick up the family, the cot and the presents and return by car to our flat in Battersea before the first duty sometime the next day.

I actually had more time to get settled back to Battersea than I first thought for I was to report for night duty, which meant parading at 9.45 p.m. the next day. When I arrived, with some nervousness, I realised that in future I needed to be ready long before the fifteen minutes parade-time. Fortunately another sergeant also new to the division had arrived before me and got the

Duty Board (parading up to fifty constables at separate times) sorted out.

'Welcome to the madhouse,' Inspector Frank Gutsell told me. 'Glad to know you're a rugby man. With your height we can do with you in the scrum.' He then added, 'Robin, don't go out yet; there are twelve waiting to be charged and you have a good jailer. He'll give you all the help you need.'

So on the first night I didn't actually get out to walk around Soho until after 4 a.m. – by which time I was reeling with tiredness having not slept the day before. Then I had to come back in soon after 5 a.m. to complete the 'State' – the large duty book logging where every officer had been posted, that those on leave and on courses were accounted for and so on.

While the sergeants' course at Hendon had given a good ten-week preparation in the late autumn, it was now real, actually happening. Within those first few weeks, it was a real joy to go on duty at whatever time – so much to do, so much to continually learn and so much fulfilment. One of my sergeants from 'D' Division days was now an inspector. My older colleagues had warned me that Mr Ingram would rarely walk by himself and usually collared a sergeant to walk with. I knew this, anyway. So one night, after parade, when he invited me to take a walk with him, I wasn't surprised. His explanation was that a new strip club had opened the previous weekend and we hadn't yet visited it. We needed to know where the exits were, who the staff were and so on for future reference.

We looked here and there but took some time to find a very narrow alley just off St Anne's Court in Soho.

'Ah, this is it; come on, Robin, let's see what we can find.'

We walked along the alley, and came to some steep steps – a fire escape – with open doors at the top, a curtain fluttering in the breeze, and much music from within. Up the steps we went, and Mr Ingram walked through the curtains to find himself on stage with two completely nude writhing females. They were so surprised but turned it into their act as they wrapped their legs and arms around him; the punters thought it was part of the show and were yelling 'Get 'em off!' (his clothes not the girls). I was in stitches, watching through the curtains. He took some time to extricate himself and the howls could have been heard in Piccadilly Circus as he fell outside.

'Robin,' he said, 'I want a word with you! Why didn't you follow me in?'

Talking of strip clubs, there was good reason to raid them on occasions – not a pleasant duty (especially as it often meant confiscating larger than life-size photos of females in various poses with little or nothing on). I remember one just off Shaftesbury Avenue which abused its hours of opening, its licensed bar and so on. I was deputed to lead the raid and, having deployed my officers and gone in at the appointed time, I went to the manager's office. Apparently not at all surprised, he stood up behind an untidy desk, and greeted me warmly: 'Hello, Robin! What can I do for you?'

I had a policewoman with me who seemed somewhat astonished.

Actually, he was the incumbent manager of the New Scotland Yard restaurant in the day-time and, of course, I knew him well. Needless to say, he had completed his last duty there!

Another inspector I found myself walking with was a Mr Caligari, who was new to the division and glad to have some company. We were in Wardour Street – a gaudy, crowded and noisy place just up from Old Compton Street. We could hear another noise above the normal buzz and, from a side turning a Rolls-Royce appeared, moving very slowly, with a huge crowd of screaming teenagers clinging on to it. It was the Rolling Stones, already great idols. I thought I remembered that one of them had just been dealt with in Liverpool for having no insurance while driving the car and it was enough for us to stop it and see who was at the wheel. What a mistake. Neither of us knew one from the other; I had no real idea if the rumour was right and, in any case, trying to get them to produce documents would have been impossible. Then Mr Caligari seemed to get engulfed by the teenagers and I saw the boot of the Rolls-Royce open and him scrabbling about amongst dozens of others, trying to pick up some of the fan mail which had spilled out. Mr Caligari, a stamp collector, got his worth, the girls got their kisses from the Stones and I just laughed.

I was selected – probably the wrong word as the captain was struggling for anyone who might be able to catch a rugby ball – for the 'C' Division rugby team, and we had some great matches. Rank means nothing on the field, and Frank Gutsell, the fly-half, encouraged that for everyone. It was against a Plymouth side that for the third time my nose was broken and, as a result, my nickname (Forty Towers) changed for some weeks to Basher, as my nose looked like that of Brian London, the former heavyweight boxer (Basher was his nickname). In that team were two Christian men – Brian Brooke and Johnny Pridmore; both were outstanding encouragements to me as a sergeant and as a colleague. I well remember the day when Johnny became a Christian, his delight, and the wonderful change in lifestyle which others in the team and the station recognised immediately.

Cricket was also on the menu and there were plenty of games to be had – though, again, our home ground at Imber Court (same as the rugby ground!) was often further than our away fixtures. Getting off for sport was always a problem, though at West End Central there were plenty of opportunities to swap duties with colleagues.

Chris had continued to work at St Thomas's Hospital, firstly as charge nurse in the Psychiatric Department and, later, as charge nurse and acting Sister in the Sexually Transmitted Disease Department. She would push the pram with Steve the three miles to the hospital and keep him in the department with nurses taking their turn to cuddle and feed him – he wasn't that thrilled in later life when we told him that he spent the first twelve months of his life in a VD clinic.

Chris left St Thomas's in June 1963 and in August, our second child was born – a lovely daughter, Judith Christine (Judi). But two children in our small Battersea apartment was a bit tight.

It was about this time that the former headquarters of the Christian Police Association moved from Dennison House in Vauxhall Bridge Road, Victoria, London. The new director was the Reverend Peter James, a visionary and energetic rector from Little Leighs in Essex. His parish was relatively small and he was able to combine the two jobs, having the national office in his rectory. One of the council's first changes in direction was to establish branches to coincide with police force boundaries. London became one of the first to be set up under this idea. For whatever reason, I was appointed branch secretary. We began monthly evening meetings in the London

City Mission headquarters, near Victoria, and published a newsletter which was informative for members and (we hope) a challenge to non-Christian colleagues.

A great help to me was Brian Eales, that giant of a man at six foot seven and around twenty-three stone! He was the Acting Sergeant in 'A' Division section house in Ambrosden Avenue; also Jim Green, an inspector at Paddington and, for two periods, at Hendon. They both taught and encouraged me, and gave much advice; they were very patient in those early days, as were Frank Lording and John Barratt, who were recently retired.

We still went out on team-work – one visit in particular sticks in my mind. Ron Perrett and I travelled to Great Wakering in Essex; Brian Eales had hoped to be with us but was prevented from coming. The church we were visiting was called The Peculiar People and we arrived by car at 10 a.m. for the 10.30 service. In the vestry, we apologised for the limited size of the team; our instructions were to finish dead on 12.30 p.m. as the local hourly bus stopped outside the church at 12.40 p.m. Two hours to fill! I had a children's talk with an Egyptian water pot which normally took about eight minutes but, with much prayer and trepidation, I was able to make the pot last for twenty minutes without drying up. Ron was leading and preaching, I gave a lengthy testimony and we lasted it out. When we asked about Sunday school, the elder said that it started at 2 p.m. and finished at 4 p.m. with the evening service at 6.30 p.m. until 8.30 p.m. Six whole hours of mission . . . was it impossible? We prayed – a lot – and, with much singing and long preaching (forty-five minutes at least) we managed it, but were glad that we weren't the minister having to do this every week.

At West End Central, I had one very difficult matter to deal with concerning a Christian constable. In those days one of the great Acts of Parliament that permeated policing, along with the Metropolitan Police Act 1839, was the Vagrancy Act 1824. Yes, it was very dated but Section 3 gave power of arrest of all sorts of layabouts who littered the streets, including beggars. It was unique because the power to arrest a beggar was not optional. Most powers of arrest used the word 'may' and so give an option of summonsing but this used the word 'must'.

My Christian PC was in Oxford Street and received several complaints of a scruffy, smelly beggar accosting people for money or drink. The constable found the man with a plastic cup but, instead of arresting him, gave the man a couple of quid and sent him on his way. Inevitably, complaints came to the police station about this and, because it was known that he and I were members of the Christian Police Association, I was given the task by the duty officer of dealing with it. I spent some time with the complainants and assured them that I would deal properly with the matter.

When I spoke to the constable, letting him hear the complaints, he immediately realised that he was wrong but said he had felt that arresting the man would do no good at all (incidentally, giving him money did no good either). I had no option but to report him but there were also questions about his assertiveness and I asked him to really consider whether he was convinced that his proper calling was to be a police officer. Some days later, he came to me with a letter of resignation – which I believe was the best option. He subsequently went into the ministry and became an army chaplain – still a tough job, but perhaps with fewer dilemmas for the Christian.

It was at West End Central that I first came across Freemasonry; for some five months, I was on a special job with a chief inspector and worked closely with him in his office. He knew of my Christian faith and never once tried to compromise me or criticise my stance. He was, however, an ardent Mason, and all too often – too many times for it to be a careless mistake – he would drop literature near me about Freemasonry. He would never give away the secrets but more than once offered advice that if I wanted to get on it might be wise to follow in his steps. I knew little about it so went to a book shop in Tottenham Court Road to buy books on the Craft, merely to see what it was that he was so keen about.

A matter of days later, I was met by two other senior officers.

'We hear you've been buying books on Freemasonry. Why? We want you to give them up and we'll get your money back.'

Wow, was there a threat here? Needless to say, I still have the books; I read them and was very surprised by what I discovered. It never entered my mind to spill the beans to others (which is what the senior officers were worried about, I think) but I could see absolutely no reason to join. Yes, perhaps I took a risk but as far as I know it never hindered my future and the subject was never mentioned again while I was at West End Central.

While I couldn't match my Christian faith with the principles of Freemasonry, my friendship with, and often admiration for, colleagues who were 'on the square' was never a struggle nor a compromise. Of course the temptation was there because it was rumoured that promotion was often made easier if it was known that one was an active Freemason. I have to say that that was only a rumour; I was never fazed if a Freemason was promoted or given a specialist job, neither did I ever think that it was because of that allegiance that they got the job. This isn't the place for me to go into why I felt it was not for me but it does give me the opportunity to say that my God is bigger than any society membership, and if I were to be promoted – or, indeed not promoted – it was in greater hands than mine.

Generally speaking, officers at West End Central were hard-working and conscientious and there was much humour. One morning, I stood with another colleague at about 10.45 a.m. in Piccadilly Circus. One of London's busiest junctions – Piccadilly, Regent Street, Shaftesbury Avenue with the Eros monument in the middle, the area was a real tourist attraction. On this particular day, an American couple spoke to me, presumably because I had the stripes and rank, to ask me the way to Birmingham. I was about to say, 'Get to Euston Station and catch a train' but my colleague intervened and said, 'Whereabouts in Birmingham?'

'Well, just outside Birmingham, Sutton Coldfield.'

'Do you know the street in Sutton Coldfield? And the house number?'

They told him.

'OK,' said my colleague, 'I'll write this down for you. Go round the corner to the second bus stop and catch the 159 to Euston Station. Go to the ticket office and book your tickets to Birmingham New Street. There's a train at 11.50 a.m. When you leave the station by the north exit, turn right, and at the bus stop wait for a number 30A – a green single-decker – and book to Doe Bank. Ask the conductor to put you off. When you get off, turn right and then walk about 150 yards and the house is on your left.'

It was then that I heard someone say, for real, 'Aren't British police wonderful!'

Stunned, I turned to my colleague and he shrugged. 'Coincidence. My parents-in-law live just next door!'

10.

The time of my life

One of the jobs for sergeants was visiting licensed premises – known as 'doing the cards'. Each month, the sergeants had a card with names of licensed premises to visit to see if the law was being kept, there was good order, they closed on time and so on. It was a good way of getting to know the licensees and their staff including the doormen. Each theatre had at least one bar which had to be visited and it was possible in the month to visit it at consecutive times so that one saw the complete play or show and oversaw the licensed bar at the same time. The cards were especially good for rainy days and evenings.

With the sex-trade in both Mayfair and Soho, there were many problems when eminent and well-known people were involved. At times it was embarrassing both for them and my officers especially when the press cameras arrived! And speaking of embarrassment . . . Once, my mother was a patient in a London hospital. She had a loud-mouthed and unattractive prostitute in a bed opposite. And when I went into the ward, this girl suddenly shouted, 'Hey, Robin! Come to visit me?'

My mother looked shocked.

Actually I didn't recognise the girl at first as she had a birthmark across one side of her face which, presumably, with cosmetics, she was able to hide when on the streets. The fact that I failed to realise who she was made the situation worse as she recounted the number of times I been with her . . . she didn't mention that I had arrested her! My mother was appalled.

On another occasion, I had an experience in Soho which caused much debate with my fellow Christian police officers. A businessman, in London from out of town, had a heart attack and died while naked with a prostitute in Berwick Street, Soho. The ambulance crew tried to revive the man, and very considerately put some of his clothes on the body but would not take it away. It took some time to get the divisional surgeon to pronounce death from natural causes, then for an undertaker to arrive; the prostitute, though a little shaken, seemed more concerned about the interruption to her takings.

I wrote my report and discussed the detail with my colleague, the coroner's officer. The man's wife came to London next day and met us at the police station, obviously wishing to know the circumstances of her husband's death. I was trying to be sympathetic and helpful but it wasn't in my heart to say that he died having intercourse with a prostitute. I simply and quietly said that he had collapsed in Berwick Street. His wife, fortunately, didn't ask me why he was there or what he was doing. At the inquest, following the post mortem, the coroner – who knew the details of the man's death – questioned me in the witness box and, as was usual in those days, led me in my testimony.

'And did the deceased collapse in Berwick Street, officer?'

'Yes, sir.'

He also spared worsening the grief of a lonely widow.

The discussion to which I referred was a very meaningful debate about lying; some took the stance that a police officer should *never* lie – it should be the truth, the whole truth and nothing but the truth. I was taught that at training school and fully adhered to it but wondered if there should be exceptions. In the debate, I quoted the above incident and Detective Inspector Peter Langley from Special Branch referred to a time when he acted as a waiter to listen and watch certain individuals. Someone had whispered in his ear, 'You're the Old Bill, aren't you?' Peter had to deny it otherwise the job would have failed. In police work, in its many wide and varying aspects, there are occasions when the question of complete honesty has to be compromised, for example, when the end justifies the means – but it is a very touchy subject.

Dealing with vice isn't easy. This is not a cosy and gentle lifestyle for the girls; they are usually at the mercy of their pimps and, of course, they don't know most of the men who pick them up; these men can be violent, abusive, depraved and heartless. Many of the girls in Soho worked from seedy, badly furnished rooms with bare light bulbs. I knew of a prostitute who, at nineteen, was thoroughly miserable and depressed; one of my Christian colleagues gave her the address of a Young Women's Christian Association hostel some way away. She knew the risk of reneging on her 'handler' but went for it. She cried for days, apparently, but gentle counsel and the love of Christ from some of the staff enabled her to see that there is a better life for a young woman and she became a Christian. She was able to contact two of her prostitute friends who came to join her at the hostel and they, too, desperate to find another life, became Christians and were nurtured at a nearby lively church.

Some time later, they were bold enough to work the streets again, not as prostitutes, but with the aim of reaching their former friends – a sort of missionary work; and what better missionaries than those whose lives had come from that dark background?

Working in Soho and Mayfair was 'the real stuff' for police officers. I enjoyed the variety, the glitz, the jazz clubs, the restaurants, the theatres and, of course, dealing with the crime. One evening I had an urgent signal on my pocket radio to meet PC 199 in Wardour Street where he was involved in a fight. As it happens, I was only in Shaftesbury Avenue – doing my cards – so I ran into the centre of Soho. There was a fight all right, but PC 199 was nowhere to be seen. I waded in thinking that he might have been knocked to the ground, being trampled on by a dozen or so drunken thugs. I was getting pushed, punched and kicked and was shoved into the doorway of a coffee bar. Fending off blows, I went in backwards. I was up against a wall but it was only a plywood façade. Pushed through it, I fell backwards down a short flight of stairs. The yobs didn't follow but there I was, no helmet, in torn and filthy uniform and thoroughly unkempt . . . in a Chinese gambling den. I had knocked over a sort of mah-jong table, scattering a number of people who mysteriously found a way out; I struggled to my feet and, in a deathly hush, faced a number of very angry (and well-dressed) oriental men, plus some scantily-clad young ladies.

I tried to become dignified.

'Who's the man in charge?'

They all feigned not to speak English. So I slunk out and, back at the police station, left a note 'of interest' in the Clubs Office, the specialist unit dealing with vice.

PC 199 and I met later in the night. He said he had not been prepared to get stuck into a fight with so many against him so he radioed for assistance and said he waited but nobody came before the fight broke up! When he saw my appearance, the grazes on my face, he then told me, his sergeant, 'You were foolish to get involved!'

'I went in to rescue you, mate,' I said. And marked his card for future reference.

Some time later, I was walking through Greek Street; it was cold, windy and not very crowded, which was unusual. Just ahead of me, I saw PC 199 with a young couple. The couple had been assaulted and the woman had had her handbag stolen and two rings snatched off her fingers, and the man had had his wallet pinched from his overcoat pocket. They had both been injured in the scuffle which they said has happened a few minutes before in an alley off Charing Cross Road.

We got a description of two men in their twenties and a girl, perhaps a bit younger. The description of the men's clothing – and they were perhaps the first ever 'hoodies' for they had their heads covered – was nothing special; dark clothing, not well dressed; however, the girl was more distinctive with long blondish hair, wearing a red or light brown jacket over a white blouse and dark mini-skirt.

I radioed for assistance, giving details of the three, and told 199 to take the couple to Charing Cross Hospital and to wait there until CID arrived. Soon I had a number of officers to help in the search, and the area car. We spread out but had little hope of catching the robbers. I wandered around and, stopping outside the familiar green double doors of the billiard and snooker club, walked in. I went up the stairs into a crowded room, dark except for lights over the eight or so tables. I spoke briefly to the doorman, who I knew as a helpful guy, but he said that he hadn't seen any non-members, although he had been on his break until fifteen minutes before.

I asked him not to draw attention to me; I gave him my helmet and my overcoat and asked him not to let anyone out yet. Then I started to crawl under the tables. One or two noticed me but didn't seem bothered. I got across to the corner and was actually wondering how to get back to the door – crawl under the tables again or just get up and walk – and, as I hesitated, something dropped in front of me . . . a lady's high-heeled shoe. I knew this was a men's club so a lady's shoe was out of place. I thought I'd better get some assistance before trying to make any arrests. I really believed that all three were in there.

So I crawled back to the door, and asked the doorman if there was another way out.

'Yes,' he said, 'but I'll get my mate to seal it.'

I stood just outside and radioed for immediate assistance but no car horns or any noise. It seemed an age but, in fact, in a few minutes I had three uniformed lads and two aides to CID itching for an arrest. In we went, the officers dispersed with a rough description of the trio. Then, I had the lights up throughout the snooker hall; the surprise and hush of the players and audience was stunning. I headed for the corner table and crept underneath to see the shoe still there – and the young lady and her two friends hanging there like fruit bats! I yelled to my colleagues to come and 'assist' them out as I said my piece, 'I am arresting you three for suspected robbery' and I cautioned them together. They were searched and the handbag and wallet was found – the rings were discovered in one of the shoes later. They didn't struggle and a gangway of humanity opened up as we led them out into the street. There was a round of applause from the punters in the snooker hall – and a few jeers out in the street.

West End Central gave a wonderful variety of police work – for some months I was the immigration officer seeking out those who had overstayed their welcome; some whose papers were incorrect but were legitimately in the country; some 'illegals' involved in crime; some who had contacts in high places and threatened me with a whole number of Lords and Ladies who might bring my job to an abrupt halt. I also understudied a colleague as firearms officer looking at licensing, collection of antique weapons and so on. I was already a marksman, so had a great interest in this other side of the 'sport'.

The main people I mixed with were, of course, the sergeants. We had a separate canteen, and we swapped experiences every time we had refreshments. I remember one breakfast-time there was an air of despondency. David Howe, a long-serving station sergeant, had had a Promotion Board the previous week and had been quite optimistic about his chances, but that day had received the notification that he was not selected to be an inspector. We were trying to commiserate with him but the conversation stopper came from Stan Walton.

Stan was an extrovert character from the East End, a real cockney. He was drinking his tea – he never lifted his cup from the saucer but bent down to table level, tipped the cup and slurped. He looked over his cup and, spraying tea everywhere, announced, 'The trouble wiv you is you ain't got no bleedin' culchure.' There was a stunned silence before we all burst out laughing. Stan was not amused – but it cheered David up.

Demonstrations and riots! I was now right at the centre of them – in Grosvenor Square with the American

Embassy under siege – and we didn't have any sort of protective clothing in those days. In one of the melees in Grosvenor Square, I had the painful indignity of being injured by an outraged police horse which stamped on the same 'gravestone' foot. The demonstrators were pushing knitting needles into the horses' rumps and throwing marbles under their hooves. I have already mentioned Red Lion Square – a student was killed in a rush trying to break the police cordon. That was an awful and painful day to remember – many of us were injured. But most of the marches and demonstrations were peaceful; some noisy and some quiet. It was a time to speak with those taking part and listen to their views and reasons for making their point. Many of these duties fell on a Saturday or Sunday so sport and church were frequently interrupted.

Then there was the pageantry – Opening of Parliament, Trooping the Colour, Lord Mayor's Parade and so on; while not in 'C' Division, we were providing extra personnel for 'A' Division. On one 'Trooping', probably June 1965, I had twenty officers in The Mall and met Chris and my young son, Stephen, in his pushchair – it was pre-arranged! I always encouraged my colleagues to be friendly and make way for children and the elderly to be at the front of crowds so it wasn't out of character to pick up Steve and put him on my shoulders. He shouted and hollered with the thousands of others and was convinced that Her Majesty turned to look at him and wave her hand when he yelled, 'Hello, Queen.'

Promotion was another part of being at West End Central. It was a wonderful place to be, but even better to be out of it in the next rank. That meant studying hard to pass the exam first time. Today it is called the Inspectors' Exam but then it was the Met's peculiar rank of station sergeant

(Dixon of Dock Green had that rank) with three stripes and a crown above. I was determined and policing in all its aspects was interesting so study was not really a chore. Eventually the examination day came and six weeks later I had the notification of success ... then remembered that there was a second part to the exam – an oral test in New Scotland Yard. That really was daunting – three very senior officers handed the candidate a board with a number of detailed questions – 'Please answer them in any order you like' being the only instruction. However, I was relieved see my name in *Police Orders*; I had passed the tests with about twenty-five others. What a hurdle to get over! I thought it was the last examination I would ever take. How wrong I was.

I went off to Hendon for the Station Sergeant's Course of six weeks. Then I was approached by Superintendent Frank Dodds of the training school. He had been part of the panel to hear one of my presentations on the course. He wanted to know if I would consider being an instructor. I felt that if this was of God, I would pass the course, which was starting about a month later.

So, I went back to Hendon to be taught how to instruct. I enjoyed it and felt more and more at home as the days went by; I was pleased to find I had passed. Then, incredibly, in *Police Orders*, on the same day, was my posting as a station sergeant to 'E' Division and, in the mail at West End Central, a letter from Mr Tommy Walls, Head of Training, to invite me for a month's trial at Peel House Training School! I went to Tottenham Court Road the Friday before my starting date, and met the Chief Superintendent who knew already that I was having a short secondment; I was given a locker and met a few new colleagues, then took the weekend to sew on the crowns above the three stripes before reporting to Peel House.

It was now more testing; a policeman with even more rank, expected to lead, to make decisions – but there was still the same thrill of being part of London's police. I was still proving Gilbert wrong, and having the time of my life.

Then Sue was born – the tiniest of the three and our flat was too small too!

11.

More challenges

I never actually worked at the new station. From that month's trial at the training school, alongside an established instructor, taking more and more of the lessons, I was taken on the staff without returning to division – the beginning of a completely new style of policing with a very happy crew, all of whom were so willing to help. News had reached Mr Walls, though, that I had worked in Scotland Yard and it wasn't long before he called me to his office to tell me that I was to be the stand-in for his clerk if ever he was on leave or sick. I smiled when he said to me, 'Sit down, son; here, copy my signature in case I'm out when I need to send a memo.'

I was teaching new recruits, firstly for the first four weeks of their careers – the Junior Stage; then a different class for the next four weeks – the Intermediate Stage; and then, another class for the last five weeks, the Senior Stage. For lecture notes, we had some sketchy guidance but we were expected the make 'spreads' in a different coloured folder for each stage, with plenty of illustrations for the classroom and many practical exercises in the parade yard. There was also much fun especially when colleagues, who had free periods, would be asked to act as stooges for the practical exercises – to act drunk, to put up a mock civil dispute, to be drivers of vehicles as we set up an accident and so on.

It was about this time that Chris and I decided to move into police accommodation because of our growing family. We went to live in Peckham – actually opposite the park called Peckham Rye – a three-bedroom flat. We soon linked with Rye Lane Peckham Baptist Church; Superintendent Rupert Horne was a deacon there. After our move, our youngest and second daughter was born, Susan Elizabeth (Sue). When Sue was dedicated at church, Steve, aged three-and-a-quarter, escaped from our clutches and amused the congregation by running around, peering through railings on the podium and making faces at the congregation. Mr Horne said to Chris, 'He'll be lovely when he's eighteen!' And he was.

So I had a double life; in the evenings and at weekends I was trying to be a husband and a father and, during the day, teaching and acting as a stooge, even as a criminal. I recall having been asked to be a drunk-driver in a lesson, firstly when the instructor showed how it should be done, and then with each recruit. I am not a natural thespian but I had several memories of dealing with such arrests at both St John's Wood and in the West End, so I did what I could. At one point, when a recruit was being rather timid, I began to fall about and tripped myself up, banging my head on the car bonnet. With blood oozing from my forehead, my speech was now incoherent. It was then I heard one of the class say to his mate, 'Blimey, he is drunk; fancy going that far.'

One of the instructors was a former rear-gunner of a Lancaster bomber in the RAF during World War Two. Ivo Wheatland was a real character, a little older than most of us, and a good instructor. However, his one failing was that he thought he knew the Instruction Book well enough not to have his own notes.

Ivo usually took the Intermediate and Junior Stages but, due to someone's compassionate leave, he had to do a week with the Senior Stage. A colleague of ours had apparently noticed that Ivo was to teach 'Drink Driving' (which is quite demanding and precise). When Ivo wasn't in the staff room, this colleague turned to the rest of us.

'Ivo will be in soon,' he said, casually, 'and he'll ask for some notes. I'll give him my file.' So, when Ivo returned, our colleague volunteered his file, and that was that. Or so it seemed. In truth, we had a feeling something was up. But we didn't find out what had happened till later. Our colleague had doctored the notes. The first two pages gave the normal lesson but halfway down the third page, he had written: 'Now, there are ten points you must note for this enquiry. Each is most important and I have made them out as an acrostic so that you can remember them.' Ivo had turned to page four – but the next page was blank except for the words

Over to you, Ivo.

No doubt Ivo got his own back. But I noticed he never asked to borrow another set of notes again . . . Training school; I remember the tremendous camaraderie, as well as the demanding days. It was always great fun. Seeing raw recruits become presentable and confident constables and, later in life, reading of them in *Police Orders* and seeing them do well by specialising or being promoted was immensely satisfying.

It was during this time that the Billy Graham Crusade of 1966 came to London. I had been invited to sit on the organising committee and, as I was a serving police officer, asked to look at security in and around Earls Court and get a team of duty police officers together to be available each night within the stadium. It was a daunting task but I saw the local Divisional Commander in 'F' Division and let him know of my role, and also amazed him by informing him of the expected numbers who would be attending for the crusade. He would police with extra numbers outside Earls Court and its surrounds and I would, with colleagues from the Christian Police Association, look after security and good order inside.

It meant a daily rota of twenty-five Christian colleagues – of all ranks – melting into the crowds on the top, middle and ground floors, patrolling the immense spaces surrounding the arena, and looking after the offertory each night (which amassed thousands of pounds). We also had to be very sensitive with the people who came. Some were very emotional, others very exuberant; we had to attend to high-profile personalities who were invited (it was where we first heard Cliff Richard give his testimony) and, as an absolute priority, we had to ensure that no intruders invaded the auditorium. Wonderfully, with very few incidents, and with much prayer, it all went well and a number of police officers who attended as guests began to live a new life in Christ on and off duty.

Now, as a family, we had moved house to Grisedale Gardens, Purley and returned to our old church where the Reverend Frank Cooke had been inducted. He and his wife, Bette, became our good friends. I was elected to be a deacon amongst some very wise and older menfolk. So, we had a wonderfully challenging two years and then came a sudden shock. Mr Walls bowled into the staffroom one day and just pointed to three of us and said, 'I've put you up for the Inspectors' Board next week. Don't let me down.'

So there we were, a few days later, in full uniform marching down Regency Street to New Scotland Yard for the ordeal of long interviews on which our futures depended. At least we had got used to the sound of our voices and the need to think while we were speaking, so that was a distinct advantage. One of my colleagues had the dreadful embarrassment, following his interview, of getting up from his chair to leave the room, opening a door and finding himself in a cupboard.

I was asked some scorching questions about the principles of policing, what the future might hold, were there any improvements to be made and, of course, the inevitable, about my Christian faith. The day before the Board, I had been to the casualty department of Westminster Hospital with an excruciating pain in my right calf muscle; after an X-ray and much discussion, a deep-vein thrombosis was diagnosed and the doctor wanted to admit me immediately. Having waited for this offer of promotion, I wasn't inclined to miss out so, having signed a form which stated that if I died it was my fault and not that of the hospital, I walked – or rather, limped, out of the hospital on the promise that I would return next day. My father-in-law, hearing of this from Chris, waited outside Scotland Yard and personally escorted me to the hospital following the Board. I was incarcerated there for the next week.

Ten days later, when I was back on duty, I found out that I was to be promoted. I was very fortunate to have been nominated to attend the six-month Inspectors' Course at Bramshill. That was due to start in early April, only three weeks ahead. So here I was, only in my ninth year as a police officer, just about to be made inspector.

I was measured for my new uniform at the clothing store but just one week before I was due to leave for the police college, it was not ready. On the Friday (I was to go to the college on the Sunday), I was called to Lambeth Store and fitted with a uniform which had the insignia of a Commander. It fitted perfectly . . . but it belonged to the infamous Commander (later Sir James) Starritt. The storeman said it was all right and coolly snipped off the laurel wreaths and put in the inspector's pips! I thought there could be trouble here. Sure enough, while in my first week at Bramshill, I was called to the telephone to hear the angry voice of Commander Starritt. Suffice it to say that he was not impressed – even less so when I tried to lighten the conversation by saying that I would look after it for him. Most of his noise was bluff, as he later admitted, but it was daunting at the time. I later learned that he had seen the funny side of it all. But he never let me forget that I had had his uniform. He mentioned it, without fail, every time I spoke to him. And his final comment was always: 'I suppose you'll be wanting my *job* next!'

So now I was a student at the awesome Bramshill – the national (really international) police college. It was a real privilege to have been selected and I only knew the three from the Met out of the sixty who were on the course. We were in syndicates with two members of the directing staff, one a civilian and one a police chief inspector or superintendent from any force in England or Wales. The course had two main streams – police management principally, and topical mind-broadening! Many opportunities for sport from April to September meant cricket, volleyball, bowls and even five-a-side soccer. What a splendid place to learn skills for the future, to enjoy the company of colleagues from other forces and to broaden one's mind on current affairs; as options I took Classical Music Appreciation and the public speaking course, the latter under the tutelage of the late Dorian Williams, who was also at that time the BBC show jumping commentator.

Much serious study, good conversation in the bar and on walks, getting and keeping fit . . . and sadly, a broken ankle in the eighth week! As a rugby player, I had never broken a bone on the field (apart from my nose). I'd been asked to make up the team in a five-a-side soccer tournament. Haring after the ball I made a sudden turn, and then there was a very painful wrench and 'snap'. Hospital, plaster, crutches – I could no longer drive so had to cadge a lift home each Friday afternoon and back to college on Sunday evenings. And then, when I had the plaster removed some six weeks later, that very day I was invited to play bowls with colleagues – a game I had never tried before – but as I bent down to retrieve one of my woods, another from the next rink trapped my fingers, snapped my wedding ring and yet another bone was broken! Never believe anyone who says that bowls is not a contact game. The hospital welcomed me back on the same day.

In those days, there was a passing-out parade at the conclusion of the six months; we rehearsed marching and then the great day came. The Guest of Honour who inspected the lines was the Rt Hon Roy Jenkins MP, who was Home Secretary at the time. Tony Tisdale, the academic civilian tutor, spent some time with us all as a concluding interview, and said to me, 'Robin, your writing is not typical of a police officer. If anything, it is rather journalistic. Don't change, please. The final thing I need to say is that I have recommended you to the commandant, praying that you be selected for a Bramshill Scholarship. That means, if all goes well, you will attend university for three years for a degree. Are you happy with that?'

It was very flattering and I doubted my ability to cope but what an incredible opportunity!

It was 1967–68 and I had learnt that I would be posted to 'Z' Division on my return to the Met. Having reported to the Divisional Headquarters in Croydon, I was stationed at Sutton, 'ZS'. I arrived there on a Monday afternoon, to meet Chief Inspector Rodney Delves, who was Acting Superintendent, his boss being on sick-leave. I was given a warm welcome. And I also met 'Mad' Adams.

I'd been called back to the station following the arrest of a driver under the influence of drink. In the charge room was a man who wasn't drunk but who, from his breath, had been drinking alcohol. It was probably borderline, though the evidence of the area car crew was that the driving had been erratic. I had heard the evidence, and was considering my next action – in those days there were no breathalysers or other such equipment. Our only back-up was, if a driver was charged, a police doctor who would take a urine or blood sample. As I was thinking about what to do, the charge room door opened and a constable in full uniform, 'walked' across the floor *on his hands*, hollering like a baboon. This was my introduction to 'Mad' Adams – who, I discovered later, was attempting to get a pension due to (mental) ill-health.

At court, at the first hearing, when a remand on bail would normally be sought to await analysis of the sample, the driver pleaded 'guilty' in front of the three magistrates.

'I *must* have had too much to drink,' he said, sadly. 'I saw a policeman walking upside down in the charge room.'

Now Sutton really is in the 'sticks' but as busy as anywhere I have worked. Early on, I was called to a house with a huge hole in the roof and front bedroom ceiling – a block of ice had fallen from the sky . . . in October! I knew what to do, having taught the lesson at training school – 'ice falling from aircraft'. On another occasion, I was directed by radio to Carshalton Pond where a young lad on a motorcycle had cork-screwed, and crashed into the low railing which broke and had penetrated right through his clothing and body. With ambulance crew standing by, the fire brigade cut the boy free with about six inches of railing protruding from either side of his body. Amazingly, none of his vital organs was badly damaged and, after a spell in hospital, he was released and back to full health in no time. There were many different, interesting charges as well as the mundane; there were civil disputes, traffic incidents, and the day I had to use my car bell to race to the dentist with raving and intolerable tooth-ache. Then there was the night when a serious road traffic accident happened outside the home of the late Sir Harry Secombe. He and his lovely wife, wearing only their dressing gowns, came out to do what they could to help, supplying mugs of tea, blankets and even offering the telephone to anyone who needed to call their home.

It was during this period I was invited to be the chair of the National Council of the Christian Police Association. I found that very daunting and yet a great privilege. I was still comparatively young in CPA and could only bring a little expertise to the table – although I had been taught, at Bramshill, how to chair a meeting! I handed over the secretaryship of the London branch to Don Axcell, currently the executive director of the Association, who was then serving in the Traffic Department. Together, we organised the first 'Carols and More' Christmas celebration at All Souls Church, Langham Place in London. We asked Jack Warner, who was playing Sergeant Dixon in *Dixon of Dock Green* on TV to participate and we wrote a script for him to read, knowing that he was a renowned Christian in the thespian world. The church was packed; a great start to what became a fixture in the Met's calendar.

While thoroughly enjoying this spell of duty at Sutton, I had an unexpected telephone call from Chief Superintendent Fred Childerstone requesting me to return to Scotland Yard immediately after Christmas. The request was an order, of course, and it was a real surprise; yet another turn in a career of surprises. So it was goodbye to Sutton and 'Z' Division and back to central London. I had heard nothing more from Bramshill so I went back to 'A' Department with renewed vigour and a certain excitement. I shared an office with my former sergeant, and now inspector, Harry Mullings.

Within weeks, we had a visit from the deputy commissioner (later Sir Robert Mark, Commissioner) in shirtsleeves with braces. He asked me to put the kettle on. (Actually, there was an informal ban on kettles in offices since a trolley with tea and coffee visited each corridor morning and afternoon.)

'OK,' he said, as we drank from mugs, 'I have something very important for you both to do, working directly to me. Mr Childerstone is aware.' And he went on to outline a big challenge, left the office – and left us with our mouths open. It was certainly something to get our teeth into, and with the short timeframe – just six months – it meant long hours and many mugs of tea with the deputy. But we managed it – the start of a reorganisation of the Metropolitan Police.

The icing on the cake was a surprise letter of invitation from University College, University of London to attend for interview with Ian Kennedy (later Sir Ian). So, by the end of the summer, two things had been completed – entrance to university and the project given us by the deputy commissioner. I had to say goodbye to my

Scotland Yard colleagues – and to police duty for three years. But what an incredible opportunity to let my hair down and to study – a sabbatical! For a non-academic, this was an amazing challenge in itself. While at university, I was accepted, too, as a student at Grays Inn – one of four London Inns of Court – and completed my thirty-six 'dining-ins' during that three years.

In addition to the studies of thirteen different aspects of law – fascinating for a police officer who was used to the criminal law and minor aspects of civil law – there were also many extra-mural activities: rugby, of course, the active Christian Union, and the Debating Society, which included students from other faculties within the college. In-house debates and competitions with other universities were great fun, as were the moots at Grays Inn.

I found the work so interesting but very demanding, especially with three young children at home; I certainly was not keen on leaving Chris with all the household chores and, in any case, I wanted to be with her and help bring up the children. I was very fortunate that two members of our church – Beryl and Ray Sowden – who were working each day, allowed me to study in their home during the vacations. Yes, I did let my hair grow a little but, much more than that, I grew as a person – a mature student who enjoyed the company of those much younger than me, but who also had the privilege of listening to them, counselling where necessary and helping out. Perhaps the only slightly down side to being at university was that I was out of circulation as far as the Personnel Department of the Met was concerned. I was at college with police officers from other forces, in their respective years; all were promoted to Chief Inspector, one, to Superintendent, except the Londoners!

However, the day of reckoning came and I was delighted to have completed the course and be awarded a degree – a Bachelor of Law. The ceremony was at the Royal Albert Hall in London. Chris and my mother attended with me. It was a great thrill which, a few years earlier, I could never have anticipated or expected. The study took me out of the parameters of policing both in subject material and also in the academic approach to legal matters. I am sure, also, that it made me a deeper thinker and gave me the ability to take a broader view in debate and discussion.

The university chancellor, Her Majesty Queen Elizabeth, the Queen Mother, gave us our degrees. I saw the Dean whisper to Her Majesty as I approached her. As she handed me my degree on vellum, she shook my hand, and said, 'I understand that now you have to return to real work, Mr Oake!'

12.

Back to policing

Now it was back to policing. I had been notified that I would be working as an inspector in 'A' Division, the central division in the Metropolitan Police; I was posted to Rochester Row, which takes the south and eastern areas of the division, Pimlico included. The Chief Superintendent was Edgar Maybanks whom I knew from the adjoining section in Scotland Yard. My station sergeant, Geordie Thompson – great guy – and sergeants were all fairly young but soon showed me how good they were at their respective jobs.

My first duty, strangely, was not at Rochester Row. I had to report to Gerald Road where the duty officer had been taken ill. I was conscious of being a little rusty but at least I had remembered to have my hair cut; I was also aware that my new colleagues would be watching to see how much I knew and whether I was all brains with no bottle!

It wasn't long before my first real test came. I was patrolling in my car and, by radio, was called back to Rochester Row urgently. As I drove in, while still at the wheel, a sergeant came up to me.

'The Archbishop of Canterbury is in the charge room,' he muttered. 'It could be a bit dodgy!'

Sure enough, as I peeped through the glass of the door, there was Dr Coggan sitting on a bench; a young constable was standing nearby, writing in his pocketbook. I called him to my office; he was a probationer and this was only his third arrest. I asked for details. Apparently Dr Coggan had been drinking heavily and was in the basement restaurant of the Methodist Central Hall; while there he was noisy, he had thrown his meal against a wall and, when asked leave, had broken a table and chair in his anger. The officer had been passing the hall and was called in to deal with the fracas. Dr Coggan had been arrested for being drunk and disorderly and for criminal damage.

This was serious. I went into the front office for the station officer to inform the Press Bureau of the situation, and clear a room for a press conference . . . we'd have to inform the Chief Superintendent for him to inform the Commissioner . . . and we had to ensure complete security at the station to prevent any snooping photographer. And then for the important task – we had to have the archbishop charged. I had informed the constable that it would be very formal. He needed, formally and in the hearing of Dr Coggan, to tell me, as charging officer, exactly what had happened and why the archbishop had been arrested. I went into the charge room, introduced myself and asked the prisoner to stand in front of the desk.

'Sir,' I said, 'are you Dr Coggan, Archbishop of Canterbury?'

'Yes, Inspector,' he replied, quietly. 'I am.'

I said, 'Would you like anyone from Church House, or another colleague, a lawyer or anyone from the House of Lords to be here before we commence formalities?'

'No,' he said, 'please get on with it as quickly as possible.'

With that, I asked the constable to tell me the circumstances leading to the arrest, which he did with a little
diffidence because he was so inexperienced. When he
had finished, I looked at the archbishop and read the
two charges to him with appropriate sections. I asked
him if he had anything to say in reply.

'I am ashamed,' he said. 'I will never live this down.'

With that, the constable searched him to find only a
wallet, a cross 'necklace' and a New Testament in his
pocket with a little loose change.

I went and sat with the archbishop to try and ascertain
what had brought him to this downfall; he was very
reluctant to speak with me but I was determined to try
and discover any root cause behind his behaviour – me
counselling an archbishop! I knew that, possibly, in a
few minutes, this charge could be a magnet for the
media and become national headlines in newspapers
and be on the radio and television. I thought about praying with him in a cell, knowing that Scotland Yard was
aware of the arrest and that the media would soon be
arriving.

Within minutes, one of the 'old salts' of Rochester
Row walked through the charge room, stopped, and
looked at us sitting on the bench.

'Charlie, what have you been up to now? I like your
make-up!'

I then discovered that the 'archbishop' was an out-of-
work actor, renowned for his impersonations (and,
sadly, his drinking habits)! My senior constable had
recognised this man for what he was – an impostor –
and in a moment, the wig had come off, the glasses were
pocketed and we all fell about laughing. Was my face
red!

I actually wrote to Dr Coggan at his home address to
tell him about this incident because I knew he had a

great sense of humour. He wrote back a lovely letter and commented that the most bizarre thing about it was that it was so ecumenical – he, an Anglican, arrested in a Methodist Church and charged by a Baptist.

Central Hall fell across my path again at a later date; I was completing some paperwork in the station when a radio message to our communications room came from Sergeant Martin – a very clever and level-headed young man – asking me to meet him outside the hall urgently. To save time, I got one of the lads to drop me off. Dave Martin said to me that a Christian meeting was in progress in the main hall and twelve nuns, dressed in their black habits, were sitting in the front row of the balcony shouting abuse at the platform party. The organiser had called for police assistance and had asked them not to eject anyone or interrupt the meeting further but, as police, merely to restore order.

Normally, we would not intervene in such a case because there are very limited powers for police in such a situation. I asked Sergeant Martin how many constables he had.

'Only three who I have called from their beats, sir.'

I decided to go in with the organiser and let the nuns see our uniforms, hoping that that alone would quieten them. But as we entered the hall, suddenly we heard loud screams, shrieks and yelling . . . and then a dozen nuns were leaping down the main staircase where we tried to detain them. We managed to hold on to seven of them. We were fairly careful about how we grabbed them and were somewhat surprised to discover that we had, in fact, got hold of three ladies – and four men.

In addition to the 'nuns', a number of people were trying to get out of the building, very noisily, and there was a measure of confusion.

I shouted to the organiser, 'Why all the screaming?'

'The nuns dropped live mice from the balcony on to the congregation below!'

That was enough for me. I looked at the seven we had detained. 'You are all arrested for disorderly behaviour. Don't say anything now.' That was the best caution I could give in the circumstances. More people came oozing out of the doors, the service having been abandoned.

As the police van drew up outside Central Hall, there was cheering from the increasing crowd when the now half-dressed 'nuns' were bundled into the back of the van. As it drove off, I saw a tall, well-built man whom I recognised. I made my way through the crowd, came up behind him, firmly laid my hand on his left shoulder and said, 'Gotcha!'

He turned round. I could see his expression of horror, the blood draining from his face. He was probably trying to formulate the words, 'It wasn't me' or 'Why me? I had nothing to do with it' but he couldn't actually say anything.

I said, 'You are Kenneth Anderson from Hayes in Kent.'

'How do you know me?' he stammered.

'Kenneth, you were the commandant of Studland Bay Crusader Camp some years ago and introduced me to the Lord Jesus.'

I could see the relief in his face but he still didn't recognise me.

'I'm Robin Oake. I was born again at that camp, thanks to you and your counselling.'

In a moment, we were hugging each other and catching up on the fifteen years since we last saw each other. I daren't imagine what the emerging congregation from the hall was thinking.

I would have been glad to have had policewomen there to help but in those days, women police officers were confined to the station and not working nights; each shift for them was only seven and a half hours. They would be used when we had women prisoners, and for some other matters such as lost children. But, the great day crept up on us when policewomen were emancipated.

I was in the station office at Rochester Row when the internal door opened. Jenny, our woman sergeant, and two WPCs made a dramatic entry. Seeing me, they exclaimed, 'Sir, it's gone midnight and we're all yours!'

Wow, what a thought. It took me a little while to react and then it dawned on me that this was now 9 October 1971, when the women police section would be disbanded; now there would be no distinction in duties. But I had thought that their duties would be assigned them from the next morning. This required a bit if quick thinking.

'Sarge, call in the bobbies in Victoria Street and in Pimlico and these ladies can start their first beats with them. I'll take Jenny out.'

So that was the transition. I talked with Jenny as we drove around the sub-division; the women would now carry out eight-hour shifts, do night duty, and would have to parade with the men. Then I heard on the radio a call to our area car: 'Alpha 2, Victoria Palace Theatre. Suspects on roof.'

'Right,' I told her, 'we're going to attend. This could be your first arrest.'

I asked her to radio the station to call out the keyholder of the theatre. When we arrived, the area car was already in attendance.

'OK,' I said, 'we're going up.'

It was still dark, but dawn was about to break at about 5.15 a.m. when I coaxed Jenny on to the vertical ladder attached to the side wall of the theatre. She looked at me.

'Er . . . I'm not used to this, sir.' And she began slowly, step by step. Then she stopped abruptly when she realised that I was climbing behind her. Her hand came behind her as she pressed her black skirt against her legs.

I laughed. 'Come on, Jen. You're in the real police now!'

We reached the flat roof and my colleagues from Alpha 2 met us. 'Welcome to the top, sir.' Then, on seeing Jenny, 'What on earth are you doing here?' I suppose it was rather bizarre but it wasn't the time to have a discussion.

'I'll tell you later,' I said. 'Any joy with suspects?'

'No, sir, but we heard that the key-holder is on the way.'

'OK,' I said, 'I'll leave you up here and when he arrives perhaps you could search the theatre inside. Come on, Jen. We'll go down the ladder and get back to the nick.'

Dawn having arrived, Jenny took one look at the metal rungs, glanced at me and said, 'No, I'll wait and go down inside.'

'Chicken.' I got on the ladder.

Later, at 6 a.m., I met Jen.

'I don't think I'm cut out for this!' she said.

The Crusader camp.

Robin after winning
Victor Ludorum aged 13.

The Junior Cross
Country Team.

Robin playing rugby for the Old Reigatians.

The Colts Cricket Team.

The car which became an engagement ring.

Engagement day.

Chris nursing at St. Thomas.

Stephen aged three at the beach.

Stephen first day at St. Andrew's School.

Robin with the Duchess of Kent.

Lesley and Stephen.

The family at Buckingham Palace.

Tynwald Day on the Isle of Man.

Judi

Sue

Robin today.   Christine today.

The grandchildren.

13.

Westminster – bombs and all

Rochester Row, and indeed 'A' Division as an area, is busy not only as London's centre but also because of its political and royalty venues – the Houses of Parliament, Buckingham Palace and Clarence House – and Trafalgar Square, a traditional centre for public demonstration. But in the early seventies, there was the bombing to contend with.

In a few months, there were fifty-two live devices and over two hundred hoaxes or false alarms, mainly in connection with Northern Ireland factions. As a duty officer, this was an incredible responsibility – coping with the constant knowledge of potential high-profile targets, both people and buildings.

We got to know the bomb disposal personnel in a very intimate way because they had to trust us, the local police, and we had to have faith in them and their expertise. Most of the devices were crude and amateurish making diffusion a very dicey business. We lost one of our good friends doing this job in Oxford Street and every call had to be taken very seriously.

I came on duty one afternoon with raging toothache which no amount of painkiller seemed to touch. I thought being at work with plenty to do was better than taking a day off sick. Having just completed briefing the late turn shift, a muffled explosion was enough to alert us that another device had exploded. Sure enough, a package had gone off in the South Western District Post Office and the call came to the station almost immediately. I deployed a number of officers to the scene, briefed them about possible injuries and instructed them to put into effect any traffic diversions necessary. I drove there and discovered that there were a number of injuries but none was life-threatening. Incredibly, no one had been killed.

It took some time to sort out the mess, meet the press and get the traffic back to normal before the rush hour. As I left the scene in the capable hands of our forensic colleagues, my toothache was unbearable and at about 4.45 p.m., I went straight to Westminster Hospital having told my communications officer where I was. At reception, I sought help from the dental department; the consultant there wondered what on earth he had done to have a uniformed inspector turn up, and tried to make some jokes. Then he saw I was in agony and he said he had one student available. Together they discovered an abscess on one of my wisdom teeth and the consultant thought it would be good practice for the student to deal with it. I couldn't have cared less, such was my state. In this order, the young lad pulled the tooth out and drained what seemed like a mighty big cavity, injected a painkiller and stuffed my mouth with cotton wool. At that moment, there was an almighty crash; windows came in, car horns started blaring, fire alarms rang out . . . it was horrendous.

I didn't even excuse myself as I ran from the first to the ground floor and out into the street. It was carnage – bodies of the dead and injured, shattered glass and metal, a streetlight bent over, and a fire in Horseferry House. I radioed that I was on scene, needed ambulances and the fire service immediately, and as many police officers as possible. Soon the rush hour traffic was at a standstill, making it difficult for emergency vehicles to get through. However, some made it surprisingly quickly. Four civilians had been killed and dozens injured – some from the bomb, and most from falling masonry and glass.

I was soon filthy from the rubble, doing all I could to organise the confusion and direct operations. As the first on the scene there was no time to write anything. I assisted the injured, and helped to sift through rubble thinking, thinking, thinking what best to do with diversions, witnesses, fire appliances, the press, photographers, reporters and TV cameras. With the hospital next door, damaged though it was, most of the walking wounded went in to the emergency department and, I think, some were taken to St Thomas's Hospital.

After perhaps three-quarters of an hour, I saw the Commissioner, Sir Robert Mark, and the Deputy Commissioner, Sir James Starritt, arrive on foot and, of course, the herd of media went straight to them in Dean Ryle Street. I saw Sir Robert simply lift his rolled umbrella and point it at me some forty or so yards away. I remembered a note in *Police Orders* saying Fleet Street and Co had been advised that at major incidents, despite higher ranks being present, all questions and interviews should be directed to the duty officer. So an avalanche of photographers, reporters, microphones and cameras came hurtling towards me. Under a blaze of TV lights, I fielded the questions with the two bosses standing now not ten yards away. One reporter asked me about my facial injury and what it was like to be a victim of such a bomb attack! I wiped my face with the back of my hand, realising that my mouth was still bleeding.

Sir Robert and Sir James came over and said something like 'Well done' and 'What a day'. Sir James had his usual friendly dig: 'I suppose that's my uniform you're ruining!' I got back to the station with a fair bit of writing to catch up on. But wonderfully, I no longer had toothache.

If a device – such as a package or bag – was seen by anyone to be suspicious, the hope was to diffuse it before anyone was injured or killed or any damage caused. One bomb disposal expert, who I seemed to see all too often, knew me by Christian name. Just like a surgeon, he would always put his rubber gloves on first, give a pair to me and ask me to estimate the weight of the device. Once we had agreed on its size, I could then direct my officers to make a cordon, its area dictated according to the extremities of possible damage.

With the bomb, it could have been a surgical operation for the meticulous care the bomb disposal officers took; and I was the assistant, handing scissors, pliers and other tools in order to diffuse what were often very crude and unstable devices. Somehow, we survived.

On the subject of bombs, on night duty one evening, I took a personal call from the then Home Secretary, the Rt Hon Robert Carr. He had had an explosion at his home in Barnet but was staying at his central apartment in Westminster. He was playing cards with some political friends when I arrived but he asked me to take away an alarm which was under a doormat. This had been fitted by one of our crime prevention team, but he felt it was too sensitive. I took it back to the station and brought it into the front office. One of my sergeants thought he would have some fun and placed the device underneath the mat by the front counter. After about 2 a.m., the station had very few callers but some time later, the door opened and we heard a piercing screech and bang. The station cat had walked through the door, trodden on the mat and activated the alarm. It jumped and turned to get out but by then the door had closed so the cat bashed into it. (This cat, by the way, was useful in catching mice in the stables. It was adept at brushing itself under parked police vehicles and, being black, those who attempted to stroke it didn't see the problem until they got a handful of oil and grease.)

One of my rather different duties was the fairly frequent Sunday afternoon assignments at Speakers' Corner, near Marble Arch, where speakers of many nationalities, persuasions and religions, and those with a bee in their bonnet, would simply either speak from where they stood or bring a box along on which to stand and shout their views. It drew an incredible crowd even in bad weather because it was also a tourist attraction. There were occasions when a speaker would go over the top with their language, or issue insults or threats so they had to be warned and even removed, usually to boos and hisses from the onlookers. Perhaps Lord Soper, the renowned Methodist preacher, was the most popular speaker, and certainly the most regular. It was really rare to see his pitch empty. He was famous for his care of the down-and-outs in East London, organising shelter for the homeless, talking about the evils of drink on his soapbox, but always linking it with his personal faith and preaching the gospel. I always enjoyed listening and chatting to him when he had a pause before he was up again – maybe for a three-hour spell each Sunday.

On one occasion, during the weekend of the Christian Police Association annual meetings, I was on duty at Speakers' Corner and some of the delegates, from the

Royal Ulster Constabulary (as it was then) – knowing that I would be there – came to watch proceedings. I wished they hadn't come because even before they arrived as a group, there was an ominous stirring amongst the volatile crowd because a speaker standing on a beer crate, closely hemmed in by five henchmen, was an IRA sympathiser haranguing the government and the police and army in Ulster. The hissing and booing was coming to a crescendo when my colleagues arrived and I pleaded with them to ignore the speaker. But no, they wanted him off that beer crate. I radioed to all my officers to come and mingle with the crowd, deputing two to be with my CPA colleagues and to prevent any movement from them. I know they were incensed and they may have felt they had good reason but the success of Speakers' Corner was in permitting free speech as far as possible without reaction. The air was electric for some minutes but fortunately there was no trouble.

I had been chair of the CPA for some years when I was invited to follow Inspector Jim Green as the CPA representative on the management board of the Police Convalescent Home on the coast at Hove, Sussex. This Home, and its counterpart in Harrogate, North Yorkshire, had been founded by Miss Catherine Gurney, who started the Christian Police Association in 1883, and it was good that the association still had this Christian input. Jim had been a stalwart and was very highly thought of so to take over his chair was not an easy thing to do. Still, I was delighted to take on this role for firstly, it took me back to the Home where I spent some time following an appendectomy in 1959, and also because of the Home's Christian roots.

With the regular meetings, it kept me in touch with colleagues who had been injured on duty, or who had been ill and were convalescing. There was also room for retired officers with whom I enjoyed good company listening to their reminiscences of days in the service from all constabularies south of Birmingham.

Perhaps the highlight of these years – which included those in the rank of Chief Inspector – was the move to new premises away from the coast to Flint House in Thames Valley. Her Majesty, the Queen Mother, as patron, graciously opened the new Home and spent about four hours with patients, staff and the board of management. Her Majesty spoke with me, amongst others, but asked, 'Haven't we met before?' I said we had. Obviously having done her homework, she said, 'I think you are here as chairman of the Christian Police Association; as a fellow Christian, I applaud your work.'

It was while at Rochester Row, and living in a police house in Grisedale Gardens, Purley, that we, as a family, came home from shopping in Croydon. It was wintertime and getting dark at about 5 p.m. I sensed something was amiss because the side gate was open and I always made a point of ensuring it was closed. I asked Chris and the children to wait in the front garden while I crept round the back. There I found a well-dressed man standing on tiptoe trying to haul himself up on to a windowsill underneath a partially open fanlight. He was startled to see me, jumped down and tried to push past me. I grabbed his arm – and the screwdriver he had in his hand – and frogmarched him to the front where there was more light from the streetlamps.

Chris looked very surprised and rather scared. I asked her to dial 999. She took Sue indoors, but Steve and Judi waited outside on the lawn. I began to question this middle-aged man, who tried to make out that he was a Christian (having seen a notice about our church in the front window) and that he was looking for me. He said he stood on the windowsill to see if I was in! As I questioned him, I was beginning to catch him out and at one point, tried to get him to repeat an answer. Then Judi butted in. 'Daddy, you've already asked him that once!'

I held this man for about half an hour but no police arrived. I had introduced myself as a police inspector and smiled as he muttered, 'Just my luck.' I arrested him for attempted burglary, cautioned him before I put him in my car and, though a bit risky, drove him to Kenley Police Station, about two miles away. The man was later sentenced for other offences. If I'd been found burgling a police officer's house, I'd think the bottom had fallen out of my world.

Towards the end of my posting to Rochester Row, I was invited by the new Chief Superintendent, Mr Linnett, to take on the role of Admin Inspector again; under Edgar Maybanks, I had performed this role for a short time – it was interesting but I felt my real calling was amongst the public on the streets and commanding operational men. In fact, he had slightly changed the role and I was virtually his staff officer. Linnett was an interesting man with much energy and ability; he liked things done yesterday so it kept the staff on their toes but also made the whole station much more efficient than it might otherwise have been. It did me good because it prepared me for the next rank which was not far away. I was notified of a Promotion Board in the Commissioner's Office, with a week's notice.

The Board was chaired by Deputy Assistant Commissioner Geoffrey Dear (now Lord Dear), and his two colleagues were Commander Paddy Flynn and Chief Superintendent Peter Broderick. It was, understandably, a testing interview, not only talking about my varied career to date but also seeking my views on current policing policy and future improvements that might be made. Again, my Christian faith was discussed and tested but, a week or so later I was notified that I had passed with the date posted in *Police Orders* that I was transferring to 'L' Division, Brixton and surrounds in south London, in two weeks.

Three of the happiest memories of being a police officer were in fact from our private lives. I have mentioned that as a family we attended Purley Baptist Church and, wonderfully, first Judi and then Steve became Christians and, some time later while in Altrincham, Sue was converted. No coercion from parents but, thereafter, much encouragement!

14.

New responsibilities

I arrived at 'L' Division to be greeted by the Commander – Paddy Flynn – who flattered me by his opening remark of welcome by saying that he had specially asked for me to come to his division. It was a tough area with racial tensions and much crime; I actually went to work at Clapham Police Station to find morale low and many of my new colleagues feeling out on a limb. It certainly was a challenge but next to my office was the plan-drawer, a very mature officer by the name of Tom Millar. I soon discovered that he was also cricket secretary not only for 'L' Division but also for Number 4 District. Once again our home ground was miles away – at Hayes in Kent. But I soon found myself as the most senior rank playing cricket both for the division and the district. It was so enjoyable to get away from the office and play the game I loved so much.

Clapham had its own challenges. One day, the plain clothes sergeant came to see me.

'Sir, there's a nest of ponces in Grafton Square controlling girls in the West End; have I your permission to suss it out?' He had information that four men were controlling at least a dozen prostitutes in Soho and, while

the girls worked in central London, they were sometimes bringing their clients to Grafton Square and
neighbours were complaining. With a little more information, I agreed to let the observations officially start.
These went on for some three months and, with the
cooperation of 'C' Division, the evidence was gathered
of the girls soliciting, their clients and use of the address
in Grafton Square; watching what the men in question
were doing for a living, for income, their relationship
with the prostitutes and so on. Eventually, the Plain
Clothes Department came to brief me on the evidence
gained; it was well documented and I authorised the
necessary warrants of arrest and searching of premises.

Now, I had sought legal aid for this case – one of the
Met's own solicitors would take this case through – but
when I arrived at court to oversee proceedings, Brian
Hargreaves, whom I knew as Huggy Bear, the solicitor
and a good friend of mine through the Christian Police
Association, greeted me with, 'Ah, Robin, sorry about
this; a more sinister case has arrived on my desk which
I'm prosecuting. I've only come here to give you all the
papers while I nip off to Bow Street. Can you deal?' It
really wasn't a case of 'Can you?' but 'You will, won't
you!' So I took on the role of solicitor and addressed the
bench using the very words that my sergeant had used
to me in my office: 'Your worship, this enquiry began
with the assertion that there was a nest of ponces in
Grafton Square.' The magistrates stopped me and
queried, 'Mr Oake, a nest of ponces? I look forward to
hearing what you have to say. I take it the birds hadn't
flown?' Within moments, the press seats were full. I took
the case through – it wasn't, as they say, rocket science –
and had the case committed for trial at Crown Court.
Some months later I arrived at court and met with our
barrister, an old friend from college days and Grays Inn,

Jeremy. Then another barrister came over – another friend from college and Grays Inn. He was appearing for the defence, and when I was called to the witness box, he gave me a real stern, and emotional, grilling.

'With the irrefutable evidence my clients had stacked against them, I felt the best defence was to attack,' he explained, afterwards, apologetically.

'Really?' I said, ruefully. 'With friends like you, who needs enemies?'

On another occasion, I had to deal with two wealthy and eminent people in Streatham complaining mainly about the attitude of local police as opposed to anything specific. The Commander asked me to see these folk and get to the bottom of their comments. I arrived, not in uniform, at a pre-arranged date and time to a lovely house on Streatham Common; the lady was an eminent international opera star (I'll call her Edith) and her wheelchair-bound husband (I'll call him Bill) was a former British Golf Champion. They were in their late sixties and were rather reluctant to outline their grievance but once they spoke, I could understand why they were upset and promised to deal with it locally and report back. With that, I enjoyed a cup of tea with them and left. I called in to see the Superintendent at Streatham and he agreed to deal with the complaint.

A fortnight later, I called again to see Edith and Bill who were evidently pleased to see me; they knew that the problem had been dealt with and were most grateful. Then Edith said, 'Mr Oake, why is it that you're so cheerful?' After speaking about a happy family, my sport, my work and so on, I said that the real reason was my active Christian faith.

Although we were sitting there with coffee, friends together, Bill turned his back to me and muttered, 'Oh no!'

Edith, however, carried on. She said she had gone to church on and off all her life; she was a Roman Catholic but Bill had something about the church which he could never forgive. She said that what faith she had didn't make her happy at all; if anything, it placed an obligation on her and became a burden – just a routine she went through at church.

So I, very quickly, for I was aware that I was on duty, told her of my experience as a choirboy and bell-ringer, and the ritual of the set prayers, until I came to know Christ personally at the Crusader camp in Dorset.

'Robin,' she said, 'what a wonderful story.'

At that I said 'goodbye' though Bill had lost his tongue.

A week or so later, Edith telephoned me at Clapham and asked me to call in.

'I cannot get out of my mind what you said about becoming a Christian,' she told me. 'It must have made such a difference to you and I want to know more.'

At this, Bill wheeled himself out of the room. Edith talked about her upbringing, and her life as a star; she and Bill had led largely separate lives because of work commitments. And she said that Bill had looked forward to being with Edith in retirement but had been struck down with Parkinson's disease, deteriorating rapidly.

'Robin,' said Edith, 'I need faith; I need to become a real Christian and not pretend.' She was saying, I believe, 'I need God's grace to accept me as I am. Churchgoing alone is not enough.' It was the sort of question I loved to hear and on a later occasion I spent some time with an open Bible pointing out the way of salvation – basically, that God so loved the world, all people in it, that he sent his only Son, Jesus, who gave his life on the cross to die in our place for our sin. I talked about being born again, receiving the Lord Jesus into her life. Then Edith very simply prayed, 'Lord, come into my life; forgive me for my sin and make me what I ought to be.' I did speak to Bill too but, while he was polite, he certainly didn't want to know.

I kept in touch and Edith, as far as I know, continued at the local Catholic church where she felt at home. Then one day in the office I had a phone call from Bill, summoning me to Streatham Common. I thought the worst and wondered with what Bill was going to accuse me. I arrived and was about to ring the bell when the door opened. There was Bill, in his wheelchair.

'Robin, come into the lounge and sit down.' He looked me straight in the eye and said quite sternly, 'I want what Edith's got!' So I began to talk about God's love but he interrupted and said, 'I heard everything you said to my wife even though I had my back to you. I know that God loves me, that Jesus died for me but how do I find him?' So I knelt by Bill's wheelchair and with a great deal of emotion, led him to Christ and let him pray after me, inviting him into his life. What a wonderful solution to a minor complaint against police!

While at Clapham, I had to learn how best to caution juvenile offenders. I had never had to do that before but our Juvenile Bureau seemed to be so stretched and the policy on the division was to favour cautions rather than prosecution wherever possible. Before my first attempt at this, I spent time devising a set of words which I could use as a blueprint. I practised these on my secretary, Sue Mahalm. Her comment was 'You frightened me out of my knickers!' Well, it was meant to be scary, but I also had another plan. Would it work?

One of the bureau staff booked my first evening of cautions. Of course, they didn't know me or my method of caution so we were on tenterhooks. I confess to being a little nervous too. My first caution was of a lad of thirteen who had been shoplifting; the food had been recovered undamaged. I started my spiel as he stood in front of me; he went pale and his mother looked deeply shocked. My colleague from the bureau glared at me as if to say, 'You're being a bit harsh!' At the end of the caution, I came in with the second part of my plan.

'Right,' I said, 'that's the caution over. As far as I'm concerned, that's the end of it, but now we have to pick up the pieces.'

We talked about turning over a new leaf; about getting involved with a youth club or sport. At the end of this, the lad's mother genuinely thanked me, and the thirteen-year-old said a quiet 'thank you' and left. My colleague from the bureau escorted them out. When he returned, he said to me, 'Sir, please forgive me saying this. I really thought you had gone overboard and when the lad started to cry, I felt I should step in. But it was right because you balanced it at the end. He will never forget that caution and I'm sure his mother will be very grateful.'

The problem was that word got round and I found myself cautioning juveniles from all over the division.

Every Chief Inspector and Superintendent was required to be the divisional duty officer on a rota system which meant being on call or in the office twenty-four hours a day. On one such duty, I was working late at Clapham. I had been cautioning juveniles during the evening and was about to drive home when a call came through to the control room, and then to me in my office, that St Leonard's Church was on fire in Streatham. I chose to drive the back way to the scene, sensing that the main roads would be blocked. When I parked my car some distance from the burning church, I could see the flames coming through the high roof and thick, black smoke billowing into the sky.

As I walked towards the fire, colleagues from Streatham Police Station were already in charge of traffic control doing a difficult but excellent job; ambulance crews were standing by and the fire brigade were doing all they could to stem the fire with pressure hoses. Firefighters were on very high turntable ladders pouring water through the disintegrating roof, but the fire was too fierce for them to enter the church building so it was not known at that stage whether anyone was stranded inside. The big fear was that the very tall pointed steeple might fall. While we were able to clear the footpaths and, by loudhailer, clear the flats over the shops, there was nothing we could do about damage to any building on which it might collapse.

I found a senior fire officer who had taken charge of the scene. He was very calm and well in control of his operations. Then, like a raging bull, the chief fire officer for the district arrived, not in uniform and obviously in a foul temper. Not appreciating that I was speaking to the media, he blustered and fumed at me because 'one of your stupid and insane traffic officers stopped me for speeding and the more I pleaded who I was the more slowly he took my details!'

I tried to take him aside but the press – local, national and TV cameras – wanted this story. Strangely, he was dressed in a very loud, striped top with a casual jumper over the gaudy material; no one could have looked less like a fire chief than he did.

'What are you going to do about it?' he stormed. 'I've got this ticket and I'm on duty! I should be immune from prosecution when I'm on duty.'

I took the ticket to produce his documents from him and promised I would do something to help.

The fire was eventually damped down. No one, fortunately, was injured and the steeple somehow stayed up although it was severely damaged. The big story in the newspapers was a criticism of police for booking the fire chief for speeding en route to this serious incident and his argument with me – with photos – while the church burned down.

In addition to cricket while in 'L' Division, I was invited by the secretary to join the lads on golf days. I hadn't played the game since university. It was soon discovered that I hadn't improved much but the real golfers were very tolerant and made me very welcome. It is always a difficult balance when in a command position how far to socialise with one's officers but I tried to manage it by making the rule that we didn't talk about policing while on the golf course. It did give me the opportunity to see my officers off duty – as with cricket – and I hoped they would appreciate that I was human after all and not just a 'guv'nor'.

I had been watching, perhaps unconsciously at first as a constable, how anyone with rank acted in command; as I began to rise in the police service, I slotted those with any rank into the good, the bad and the indifferent. I could see that Promotion Boards were sometimes fooled by articulate men and women who were not necessarily good at leading. There were some who had been promoted at least one rank too many – perfectly OK as sergeants or perhaps as inspectors, but nothing further. I made mental notes of the type of boss I did not want to be and those who I would try to emulate.

So here I was at Clapham, in the first rank where I had some influence over the whole station rather than a relief or a group of officers in a section. I mentioned that morale at Clapham was low and that some of the supervising officers were in need of encouragement and motivation. I spent much time with each inspector. I met with sergeants to get to know them.

Of course, these men of rank had to trust me and see that my concern for them was genuine. As opposed to others, I made sure that my door was always open and that anyone could come and speak with me, groan at me and suggest new ideas to me. I was not always popular with the bosses to the point of being wrongly accused sometimes; I was often frustrated but still determined to uplift the personnel. That was part of the reason for playing sport; it was part of the reason for joining in social events. I suppose, in a sense, I was attempting to move from one era to another; the old system was harsh discipline which was often unreasonable – keep the bosses separate and simply direct from a distance; I sought to show the station – both police officers and civilians who also worked there – that we were a team, united together, assisting one another, encouraging one another, listening to one another, being open with one another.

One of the other responsibilities of a chief inspector was to investigate complaints against police made by the public. In an inner-city area, there are inevitable clashes with police and, at times, an officer does something wrong or says a word out of place. Most complaints were only heat of the moment affairs and many of the complainants, on seeing a chief inspector at the door to start investigations, wanted to stop it there and then, not wanting any more trouble – or even saying that it was their fault in the first place.

However, one complaint, which seemed quite innocuous when I first read it, would not go away. An argument between neighbours had got out of hand to the extent that a third party intervened and called police. A constable arrived to hear a loud argument about the use of garden tools. Apparently, one man was accused of leaping a fence, taking some implements and then using them in his own garden. The complaint was that the constable took little notice and swore at the gardeners before leaving them to get on with it.

The complaint concerned swearing, so I had to take it seriously. I eventually interviewed the constable – a man of twenty years experience in the Brixton area and certainly no fool. I had a full account of the incident which, he said, was difficult to cool as the two neighbours were so aggressive. The third party tried to intervene but he was shouted down. The constable certainly had notes in his pocketbook but when I put it to him that part of the complaint was about him swearing, especially using the 'f' word, he grinned. It seemed he had suddenly realised why they had turned their aggression on him.

The constable told me that he thought the problem was that the neighbours hadn't heard him right. Apparently the heat of the argument was dying down until he said, 'Look, let's get this settled. It's only about a fork in dispute, isn't it?'

I only had two years in Clapham before I had a call from Commander Paddy Flynn to see him in his office. Actually, my heart sank; I really thought he was going to chastise me for the way I commanded as a chief inspector. However, when I arrived at his desk, he stood up and warmly welcomed me. He opened the conversation by asking me how I was enjoying the job at Clapham; he had heard good things; he asked me how Chris was. Mr Flynn then told me that a colleague of his in A10 Branch in the Commissioner's Office had asked him how I was doing – and would I be interested in being transferred there! A10 was the Police Complaints Branch, an essential specialist outfit dictating policy regarding complaints, and taking on the investigation of the most serious complaints anywhere in the force.

Paddy Flynn's comment was encouraging: 'Robin, you've done well on "L" Division, especially by making Clapham a force to be reckoned with. Going back to the Yard could be good experience and I would back you all the way.'

As we were talking this through, sitting in his Brixton office, the Commander's telephone rang and his secretary told him it was the commandant of the police college wishing to speak with him. I couldn't hear the conversation but I think the question must have been asked: 'Do you know if Chief Inspector Oake would like to come on the staff at the college?'

I say that because Paddy Flynn casually said, 'Jim, why don't you ask him yourself? He's here in my office.' And handed me the phone.

'Hi, is that you, Robin? It's Jim Walker here. What would you think about joining the staff here at Bramshill?'

I was very flattered but, much more than that I was in a dilemma because I was wanted in A10 and the college! Policemen are trained to make instant decisions but this wasn't the time. I said, 'Sir, so good to hear you. You've given me a very tempting offer. May I ring you back tomorrow?'

I took the news home. Chris and I talked it through and we prayed earnestly together. Yes, I would love to be on the directing staff at the college but it meant a long commitment, being away from Monday to Friday each week and . . . Chris butted in and said, 'Let God show us before tomorrow night what's right.'

I returned to Clapham next day and, at lunchtime, had a telephone call from another senior officer at

Bramshill saying that he had heard I was joining the staff! Anyway, I took that as God opening a door, so I rang the Commander who said that he had informed A10 Branch of the coincidental offer and the boss there said he wouldn't compete for my services. So I went home that evening with the call from God to go to Hampshire.

15.

Bramshill

I arrived at Bramshill and thought, as I approached the old country house down the mile-long drive, 'It's good to be back.'

There was a three-week introductory course about management; then I was given a month, before my first students arrived, to prepare, to understand the nature of the six-month course, to sort out the library 'tools' that the students might need and generally settle in by getting to know my new colleagues – and, of course, move into my own office. Probably more than 50 per cent of the directing staff was non-police; there were academics, IT people, TV and radio personnel, librarians and so on, in addition to the domestic staff.

My students were all bright and optimistic inspectors; I was asked to direct Syndicate 8 (the same as that in which I studied). I was highly privileged to have the sub dean, Eric Roddick, MA MBE, as my colleague and he assisted with guidance through that first term. My students during the years I was at the college included both John Stevens (later, Commissioner of Police for the Metropolis, and now Lord Stevens) and James Hart, who was later appointed Commissioner of the City of

London Police. One of my colleagues was to become Chief Inspector of Constabulary David O'Dowd (later Sir David), so I was in good company.

I took some training at Thames TV and also with the BBC in Langham Place, London to understand something of media journalism, as well as to gain experience in interview techniques. I was also invited to join the Institute of Public Relations. One of the civilian staff who later joined us was Irene Wilson. She was head-hunted to join the staff because of her very left-wing views. Police officers need to be aware of such thinking but, in talking with her, we devised a four-hour presentation to explore left- and right-wing politics, known colloquially as the 'Beauty and the Beast' lecture!

As directing staff, we were allocated extra-curricular activities; by wonderful coincidence, one of mine was to look after the chapel – both as a place, and its services. The local vicar from Eversley came regularly to the college and was readily received; he led a communion service every Wednesday morning at 7.30 a.m. and, occasionally, some evening activities both for committed Christians in the college and as an outreach for those who wanted to know more. The commandants, under whom I served, and others such as Geoffrey Dear and Robert Bunyard (later Sir Robert) on the staff were great supporters.

The other job foisted on me was to look after the dancing class! This meant organising the hall on a Tuesday evening, seeking students of whatever rank in college each term and, the hardest part, finding female dance partners willing to have their toes stepped on. It was actually good fun and I learnt a bit myself. Sport, of course, was also high on the agenda – volleyball, five-a-side soccer and squash all the year round, and cricket and lawn bowls in the summer.

As duty officer, it was the full week Monday to Monday on call so it meant staying the weekend at college. Whenever this happened, which wasn't too often, Chris would come down with the children for a 'games' weekend. Very few students remained in-house and even fewer staff. It meant that the snooker table was free and Steve became quite proficient; the squash courts were free too, the cricket field was empty, and the bowling green was available. We had excellent free meals, and a chapel service – for perhaps a dozen or so – on Sunday morning. It was quality time for the family even though I did get home most weekends on a Friday evening.

In addition to my general syndicate duties, reports on students, encouragements and initiatives, I took on the role of TV interviewer for the Overseas Command Course, following their exercises. I enjoyed being in the studio with professional producers and camera personnel, and had the additional bonus of visiting Thames and BBC TV on a regular basis to keep up-to-date, often taking students with me for a day out.

Every other Thursday was guest night when, in the superb dining hall, students with guests would arrive first and would stand as one body for the commandant and other top-table guests. On one of those guest nights, Chris came down. I introduced her to my students and fellow staff members until I reached Charlie Abraham, a larger-than-life character from Manchester. As he met Chris, he kissed her hand and then looked her straight in the eye. 'You say you're Robin's wife? You're not the wife he had here last week!'

I was in my office one evening and researching some material on terrorism in the British Isles. It was fairly late and, as I relaxed a little, I looked at a large map of the

North Sea and mused, 'If there were to be a terrorist incident on an oil rig, I wonder which police force would
deal with it.' Sharing this with the recently appointed
commandant Gerry Lampard – Mr Walker having
retired – while at lunch next day, he thought it a good
question and that the college ought to have the answer
and give a lead. I tried the college library but there was
no guidance to be found. Looking through one book by
Professor Lipstein of Clare College, Cambridge I found
that he was asking a similar question but proffered no
solution. With appropriate leave, I made arrangements
to spend time with the professor; he answered my letter
very promptly and by telephone invited me to his study.
Together we made contact with a number of police
forces in Scotland and England and even used his contacts elsewhere in the world such as the United States of
America and the Middle East. The answer to the original
question was thought through and agreed, ultimately at
a high level. It was such a worthwhile period of study –
the academic with a practitioner and new material for
the library!

Another of my tasks on the directing staff was to ini-
tiate a public relations option. I started with a blank
sheet of paper. It took three months, on and off, to
research sufficiently and work out a programme of
study. Then I persuaded the powers that be to permit me
to start the course. I sought suitable speakers each week
to bring to my students pertinent aspects of PR which
would be useful to a police officer of middle and senior
rank. My speakers came from the Institute of Public
Relations, the armed services, industry, the media and
the Automobile Association from Basingstoke. I had the
budget to take students to the BBC and Thames TV, and
to New Scotland Yard to spend time with its PR
Department; we also went to Fleet Street and had quite

lively dialogue with journalists, sub-editors and editors. I achieved my goal of incorporating into this option the Public Speaking course which came from my own experience.

As the terms went by, the course became much more focused and relevant even to the point that some forces began to use the college for advice and direction, over and above what they were already doing.

I think the most memorable weeks that I had at Bramshill were actually spent at the Sandhurst Military Academy! The commandant had nominated me to represent the college at a leadership course for the four services – the Royal Navy, the Army, the Royal Air Force and the Royal Marines. In addition, there were non-military personnel attending – from the civil service, a financial institution and one from the police service.

As I walked up the famous Sandhurst steps between the imposing pillars, I was met by an admiral and major general, both in full uniform.

'By the size of your feet,' they quipped, 'you must be the policeman!'

Proud to be there in such illustrious company but slightly nervous, I was immediately introduced to Brigadier Peter de la Billiere who was to be my syndicate leader.

It was challenging to me as a participant, partly because I had never been in the services and also because I was well outranked. I was there to learn but also expected to challenge the service personnel with questions about their proposals and solutions from a civilian point of view. It was taxing day after day but, after the sessions, very exhilarating to mix with others socially.

One of the turning points in my career as a police officer, and also as an active Christian, was the session we had with Peter de la Billiere (later Sir Peter) who made much of the need to serve our fellow men of whatever rank. I could see that this could be likened to the high example of Jesus who said he had come to serve. The motto of Sandhurst was burnt into my mind – 'Serve to lead', from which came 'Only he who serves is qualified to lead' (voiced in syndicate by Peter de la Billiere). I made this motto my spur and, since that period at the Royal Military Academy, had the inscription on my desk wherever I served.

As my time at Bramshill drew to an end, the commandant called me to his office and asked me to give serious thought to a new project in Greater Manchester which might be 'up my street'. However, before the last guest night and the sad farewells the next day, I'd heard nothing more so I returned to the Metropolitan Police and was posted to Harrow Road just to the north-east of Notting Hill. I was welcomed there by Commander Edgar Maybanks – strange how our paths crossed so many times – and also his deputy, Chief Superintendent Derek Rosser. Edgar was warm in receiving me to his division but said that he would not be able to recommend me for a Superintendent's Promotion Board for some time as there were others already in the division who were more senior than me.

I enjoyed being operational again in a very busy subdivision, especially as the summer was upon us with demonstrations and the Notting Hill Carnival. Then, Derek Rosser telephoned me and said that he, having been on the staff at Bramshill and returning to the Met, was also penalised in the promotion stakes and did not want that to happen to me; he had persuaded Edgar Maybanks to include me in the Board the following week, going over his divisional quota. (It should be explained here that the Board in London was only for Met posts.)

Three weeks before, I had seen the advertisement in *Police Review* for the new Superintendent's post in Greater Manchester, and was interested – this would mean promotion to Superintendent outside of the Met. After praying about this with Chris, I had sent my application to be considered. As it happened, the Metropolitan Promotion Board was the day before my interview in Manchester! Fortunately, I had informed Edgar Maybanks that I had applied for the northern post so I didn't feel awkward.

I entered the room at New Scotland Yard for the Board, the 'added extra'. The chair said, 'Mr Oake, as you know, we have fitted you in at late notice. What does it feel like to be the first of fifty-eight chief inspectors to be grilled?'

'Not half as bad, sir, as you will feel having completed the fifty-eight interviews,' I replied.

There was a short silence and then hearty laughter from the other side of the table.

Again I was questioned about my Christian faith and 'Do you think that the secondment to Bramshill might have blighted your career?' At the end, I trusted that I had had good discussion but knew I was up against it having been given a last-minute chance.

The next day was the long journey north to the old Greater Manchester Police Headquarters. There I met Deputy Chief Constable Jim Brownlow (later Chief Constable of South Yorkshire and Inspector of Constabulary), Assistant Chief Constable (Crime) Charles Horan, and Chief Superintendent Albert Leach (Head of Personnel). I found this interview, although conducted in a most gentlemanly manner, very taxing and demanding.

At home, my son Stephen, just sixteen, said, 'Dad, what happens if you pass the Board in London and you're invited to go to Manchester?'

As we talked round the subject, fourteen-year-old Judi had the perfect answer. 'If you pass one or the other, you take it; if you pass both, take the one you're offered first. That will be God's way of giving you the answer!'

And so it was. I had travelled to work and was in my office when Albert Leach from Manchester telephoned me.

'Mate, you've got it. Pack your bags. You start on 4 July.'

That was about five weeks ahead. In the afternoon, Edgar Maybanks rang me to say that my name would appear next day in *Police Orders* as having been accepted for promotion to Superintendent. He congratulated me and then said, 'By the way, how did it go in Manchester?' I had to reply that I had heard that morning that I was successful. I wondered if he might have chided me for taking someone else's place on the Met Board but he didn't.

As I went home, I knew my heart was still in London with my many friends and colleagues. The Met had been very good to me and I had gained a wide experience of policing as a result. Yet something in me was excited about Greater Manchester. Obviously I shared this with Chris but waited until the children came in from school and then dropped the bombshell as we ate our meal.

'Daddy,' said Judi, 'we agreed that God's way would be that if you passed both, the first one to offer you promotion would be right. So we go to Manchester.'

And that was it – though I didn't sense much enthusiasm from Steve or Sue at the time. Anyway, a new era was beginning; another culture, a change of climate and sad departures from Purley Baptist Church, where we had so many friends. But it was exciting!

16.

Moving to Manchester

Bootle Street, the former headquarters of the Manchester City Police, was an old building with much history. Parking was at a premium and because it was (and still is) an operational station, there was constant hustle and bustle. Once I had found a space for the car, Derek Johnson, my colleague and fellow Superintendent, was waiting for me. I met Chief Constable Jim (later Sir James) Anderton in his office. I knew him well as he was the president of the Christian Police Association – and also a force to be reckoned with in British policing. He and his deputy, Jim Brownlow, welcomed me warmly.

It wasn't long before Albert Leach appeared, with his clerk, needing a few personal details for the records. He suggested to Derek that we lunched together with Charlie Abraham (who on his return from Bramshill had been promoted to the rank of Chief Superintendent in charge of the Complaints Department), which meant a lively meal-time ahead. It was rather overwhelming to meet headquarters colleagues and to travel to the various divisional headquarters throughout Greater Manchester. I didn't think my height was abnormal, but most colleagues who I met made some comments about

Londoners being tall, especially the store man who measured me for uniforms. He muttered, 'At least you 'aven't got a big 'ead.'

I had to leave Chris and the children at home in Purley because the school term had another three weeks to run; I felt so sorry for Steve because he had saved enough money – by doing a paper round, gardening for church members, and many odd jobs – to finance a trip to stay with friends in Texas. When he returned to England after five weeks, he came with the family direct to Manchester without being able to share his experience and photos with his schoolmates.

The police property we were staying in was a small, semi-detached, bare and cold house – even in September. We only unpacked the essentials. Our occupation was only temporary but it seemed interminable. We had been offered a police house in Timperley but we had to wait for our predecessors to move out. Chris was always so house proud, but now she was living in a house she could not call home; yet, she was always so buoyant when I doubted God's guidance.

We already knew of, but had never visited, Altrincham Baptist Church and made a beeline there each Sunday morning. Dr Paul Beasley-Murray was the minister and he, with his deacons, warmly welcomed us as a family. Our teenage children were soon involved with the active young people's group; this was where Steve met his future wife, Lesley.

Derek Johnson and I were largely working on our own as the Chief Superintendent, Marie Flint, was unwell and never returned to duty; Assistant Chief Constable Peter Collins, the ultimate boss, gave us our head and, so long as we kept him in touch, was happy to leave us to it. Our remit was, within twelve months, to establish a new branch so that every division had a working community contact section known in the towns and villages and well publicised in the press, and that the headquarters branch would be vibrant and an integral part of operational policing and planning.

I found the planning meetings most refreshing. I discovered that Manchester meetings were succinct, to the point and held with a ready humour.

I had been introduced to the crime prevention officer who mentioned that he was off to Partington coal mine to look at security.

'Ever been underground?' he asked me.

'No.'

'Like to come with me?'

Derek had never been to a coal mine either so it was to be a new experience for us both. Charlie Abraham also accepted the invitation. On the day, the CPO had to cry off for whatever reason so we needed a replacement.

'Leave it to me,' said Charlie. He telephoned Superintendent Ron Hadfield (later Chief Constable of Derbyshire).

'Ron, Charles here. I've got a very deep and involved enquiry on Wigan Division. I need you to come with me, now. I've already got Derek and Robin. I have to tell you it looks very black and sombre, there are a lot of dirty hands in this and it may take some time to get to the bottom of it.'

Ron arrived breathless and rather agitated. He was his usual dapper self – a light green, nicely cut suit with white shirt, stiff collar and tie. In the car, he asked many questions about what was to happen.

'Better not to know,' Charlie told him, 'better to go in cold.'

We drove into Parsonage Colliery car park. It was, by now, about 10.30 a.m. and we were to join what was known as the midday seven-hour shift. Ron eventually realised what was going on; we three had put old clothing in the boot of Charlie's car but he had no appropriate clothing! An orange boiler suit was found for him – and indeed for us all – and the manager said 'Just your underpants, lads. You'll not need any other clothes.'

At precisely 11 o'clock, we arrived at the pithead along with about twenty miners and we joined them in one of the shaft lifts. As the concertina gates closed with a sharp snap, my heart was pounding. A gentle start and then . . . we plummeted like a stone! Then rapid deceleration . . . our ears were popping.

Seven hours later, we emerged at the top of the shaft, filthy, soaking wet and very hungry. Our experience ended in the wonderful hot showers, and after that, we had a meat and potato pie. Even Ron conceded that it had been an unforgettable experience. I was so taken with it that I asked the manager if I could come again with my son. And so, about a month later, during half term, I turned up with Steve. I had warned my son about the lift and dropping like a stone so he was well prepared. He was immediately at home with the miners. We boarded an open-sided narrow-gauge train and rattled away at a very high speed to the coalface. Like I had been, Steve was amazed at the size of the mine and the immensity and noise of the coalface itself.

Having got through the pit props, we stopped for tea and a doorstep sandwich. Then I noticed the manager and the miners stirred with anxiety – they had noticed something which they didn't like and, when a distant rumbling got louder and louder, they pushed Steve and me into a tunnel wall recess. There was a sudden rush of air which became a storm-force blast, with the rumbling no longer distant but seemingly on top of us.

'It's a fall!' the manager shouted.

He urged us to kneel, hanky over mouths, and shut our eyes. My mouth was dry, my heart thumping; I could imagine injuries, being buried alive, rescue workers digging their way through to us . . .

The noise stopped as soon as it had started but the high-pitched moan of the draught and its accompanying heat was incessant. We were in pitch darkness, the electricity lines having been severed. The manager guessed where the fall had been and left us with the one miner as he went to investigate. He returned about fifteen minutes later – by now the draught had largely ceased so that the heat was almost unbearable – and said that the collapse of a gallery was not too serious but enough to block our way through. He warned us that we would now have to walk and crawl in a long detour to get round the obstruction. So we set out.

It was hot, arduous and filthy, with coal dust everywhere, which made breathing difficult even through the handkerchief.

We eventually reached a moving belt taking the hewn coal to the silo. The manager suggested that we got on this as it was also called a man-rider and would save over an hour of crawling. His one instruction to Steve and me was to keep our heads down and when he shouted, we should roll off. He had radioed ahead and at the roll-off point had arranged for two miners to hook us off – otherwise we might have gone with the coal into the silo.

Eventually we were out in the very welcome fresh air.

'Dad,' said Steve, 'I'll never go down a mine again as long as I live.'

I wasn't too keen either.

The Police Authority had obtained the lease of Chester House, Boyer Street, Trafford about half a mile north of Stretford Police Station but at least two miles from the city centre. Travelling in from the south – in fact, from all directions with the motorways – was very easy and there was ample parking space. It was a memorable weekend as we tried to locate files and other papers and get the office sorted.

Derek and I were ahead of schedule but, for some time, I was sent to Northern Ireland for an enquiry and had to leave him to it. While there, with Inspector Brian Mottram, we had a helicopter as our means of transport and a Lieutenant Colonel from the army as our pilot. On one particular day, I said to my pilot that I wanted to go to Londonderry, Lisburn and back to Belfast all in a morning. The pilot had only been in Ulster for a few days so was not au fait with the geography; we were directed to fly at over three thousand feet but on this particular day, the cloud level was low and as I was following an Ordinance Survey map, we had to fly much lower than authorised.

We arrived in Londonderry, landing in a school playground but within half an hour, the pilot informed me that unless we left within the next five minutes, we probably would not be able to move until late in the afternoon – there was a snowstorm on the way. So with hurried excuses, we jumped into the helicopter and, after a quick warm-up, took off. We immediately flew into the snow cloud. My head was down, eyes on the map and the scenery below when whoosh! – we lifted as if we had been snatched by a crane.

'What's that?' I yelled into the microphone.

'That, my dear Robin, was a pylon which we climbed over. Thanks!'

The Northern Ireland enquiry was completed after we had had alarming moments in the back of Land Rovers, and patrolling some of the Belfast streets well into the night. The shootings and explosions were all uncomfortably close but my colleagues in the then Royal Ulster

Constabulary were philosophical about it all. Without
exception they bravely tried to take the independent line
of policing without fear or favour but all knew that the
real tension was at home with respective spouses and
children who were never certain that their husband or
wife would come home unscathed after duty.

Derek and I finally presented our paper to the
Assistant Chief Constable and Chief Constable, stating
that the department was now up and running. We made
certain recommendations for the future development
which would be considered and, having completed that
job, we parted. Derek was posted north to Whitefield.

And me? I'd just received the news that the
Superintendent, Colin Rankin, had been shot at while in
his office in Moss Side. And I was greeted by the chief
who said, 'Robin, Colin Rankin has had a good spell at
Moss Side and will be moving away; this is your opportunity to put into practice all that you have promised in
the Community Contact Report!'

17.

Moss Side

My arrival at Moss Side was, I think, met with caution. 'Who is this man from London to deal with such a volatile area as Moss Side?' That's what I felt some were saying. I was shown to my office. The bullet hole was still there in the window. My first operational duty was to move the desk away to the other side of the room!

The Chief Superintendent of 'E' Division welcomed me and said he was glad I had come to the division: 'Moss Side has a bad reputation; you need to keep a lid on it. There are few people you can trust and the station is not very popular in the district.' I relish a challenge but I knew it wouldn't be easy. A number of my new colleagues had telephoned me, sympathising that I had been given Moss Side. Their comments made me a little nervous but, all in all, I knew I wouldn't shy away from the challenge of an inner-city suburb. Though quite different here in the north, I had, after all, had experience of Notting Hill, Brixton, Paddington and Camden Town.

One of the first things that happened was that I met the Divisional Commander at Maine Road Football Stadium. Manchester City were playing a home match against Leeds United. At the briefing in the shed behind

Platt Lane Police Station, there was no mention of escorting the 'away' supporters from, and back, to the railway station; no mention of a separation of supporters within the ground and, in fact, little of what I knew from my Metropolitan days of policing soccer crowds. I had been warned that Leeds supporters were mean and noisy but I wasn't prepared for the antics outside the ground before the match, and inside the ground during it.

Fortunately, the game ended in a 1–1 draw; even then, the free-for-all afterwards was almost violent as supporters of both sides merged. The Mounted Police were there in good numbers and without them we would have lost it.

I asked the boss about separation of supporters inside the ground and he said it was not done in Manchester; neither was any time given to escorts of away supporters. The next home match was against West Ham United, and it was not nearly as bad as the Leeds game; however, two weeks later Tottenham Hotspur came north and it was a real tussle to get the crowds into the ground in time – in fact, the game started fifteen minutes late.

During this game, when City scored, coins and bottles were thrown and my officers had to try to penetrate the 'standing-room only' bank. With City winning handsomely 3–0, the turmoil outside the ground and in the streets back to Manchester Piccadilly Station was horrendous. It was, in fact, the last time I was assaulted on duty and I still bear the marks on my face from the wounds. Something had to be done.

The Chief Superintendent left the division two days later on his appointment as Assistant Chief Constable, and Chief Superintendent Albert Leach became the boss. He called George Dobson (Superintendent at Hall Lane 'E' Division South) and me to his office to spend the day with him, including lunch. He said that he would be relying on us to keep him well informed. I had already spoken to George Dobson about the soccer violence and brought the matter to Albert's attention. I told him what I had been used to in London and wondered if it would work here. We agreed to meet the chief executive of Manchester City FC. We asked for strong wire netting to be hung from the rafters of the 'standing-room only' stand, and a separation gap of about ten yards either side of that netting. We would police it. We proposed to meet the main supporters' trains and escort the crowds by foot the two-and-a-half miles to the ground. We would usher them into their paddock. After the game, the away supporters would remain in the ground until it was cleared outside and then they would be escorted back to the city centre for the trains. This meant making arrangements with British Rail and also with our mounted branch boss, Chief Inspector Norman Brown; his horses would come with us both ways. It also meant a little more overtime for the constables and sergeants – but would it work?

There were a few teething problems, especially when trying to usher the crowds out of the ground and into a 'crocodile' but at least none of the stragglers of the home club could physically get at the opposition. The idea was gradually honed until we had a measure of expertise.

Soon after Albert Leach had taken charge of the division, I had to inform him that there was a widespread feeling in the community that people of Afro-Caribbean extraction were getting better housing than those of Asian origin. Three of the organisers of a protest at Manchester City Town Hall came to see me in my office and very politely informed me that they were organising a march which would start in Alexandra Park North and wind its

way through Moss Side and on to Longsight library.
They emphasised that it would be a peaceful demonstration principally to attract media attention.

About four hundred Asian people turned up that
Sunday afternoon. There were TV cameras and press
photographers, and we had deployed a sergeant and six
PCs. One of the organisers asked Albert Leach if he
could make a speech before marching and this was
agreed since the gathering was on grassland before getting on to the road. So after about ten minutes of
haranguing the city council and the county council – a
little heckling but nothing serious – Albert took charge.
He got on to the soapbox, gave a word of exhortation to
stick to the agreed route and with an elaborate wave of
his arm, as if he were on traffic point duty, the march
began – banners flying, chants of 'we want better housing' and a lot of good humour.

Albert and I were at the front leading the way when,
without warning, he turned to the marchers, put his
hand up and yelled, 'Stop!' The back of the crowd probably didn't see or hear Albert and, like a concertina,
spilled into the front marchers. I looked at Albert quizzically.

'Hang on, mate,' he said. 'I'll be back in a moment.'

He then strode across the road towards a man who
had a Staffordshire bull terrier straining on a leash.
Albert was soon speaking to the dog's owner – the dog
was, by then, wagging its stringy tail and barking like
mad at the uniform and, probably, the 400 of us watching. Albert had his notebook out and I thought, 'What's
he reporting the man for?'

Four or five minutes later, Albert came back, stuffed
his notebook back into his pocket and waved us all on
again.

'What was all that about?' I asked.

'Oh, I've got a Staffy bitch at home and I just wanted to know a bit about that dog, its pedigree and whether it might be worth breeding.'

Once, I was at home after a fairly long day. It was about 11.30 p.m., and Chris and I had just finished praying together – a habit which we have kept since the first day of marriage – when the telephone rang. It was Inspector Roy Booth. He was in charge of the Plain Clothes Department and asked if he could come to see me to sign a warrant. As he was at the station, I said that I would come in rather than have him waste time driving out to Timperley. When I arrived, he said that he had just had a tip-off about drug-dealing, that there was urgency in that the information had stated that the drugs would be distributed during the night and gone by morning and that he couldn't get any reply from the Justices of the Peace. I was the last resort!

'Roy,' I said, 'I'd like to come on the planned raid.'

'What, Sir? No! Superintendents don't do that.'

'But I do! Treat me as one of your lads and put me where I can be of use.'

So I bundled into one of the two police vans and, when we arrived, was deployed at the back of the suspected premises with a couple of other bobbies. After a long wait, presumably while Roy finalised how the raid was going to be carried out, what he wanted done with prisoners and how to conduct the search, suddenly an upper window opened and out climbed the dark shadow of a man. He slipped down a drainpipe, right into my arms. He hadn't seen us and he yelped in fright – even more so when the handcuffs were fixed to his wrists.

He started gabbling about having had nothing to do with drugs and so on – he said he was just on a 'friendly visit'. This turned out to be absolutely true. He was having an affair with his sister-in-law, next door to the house we were targeting, and this was his means of escape. Needless to say, he didn't complain about our action.

'Robin,' Albert told me later, 'you got the wrong dope!'

Still, this little episode didn't compromise a very successful drugs raid which brought in five prisoners and a hoard of cannabis.

One day, I had a phone call in my office and recognised the booming voice of Charlie Abraham. He had been transferred to take charge of the force training school at Sedgley Park in Prestwich. It was a new venture for the Greater Manchester Police who, through the Police Authority, had purchased the former Roman Catholic Seminary.

'Robin, you're in touch with God. How do I de-sanctify a chapel?'

'What do you mean – de-sanctify a chapel?'

'With the chapel as it is, there's no way I can use it for other denominations let alone other religions . . . which means I'm very restricted.'

'Charles,' I said, 'leave it with me; I'll speak to God and the Pope.'

I knew a godly man in Moss Side, Father Leigh, who I thought might help. He would have the right contacts in the Catholic hierarchy and indeed, it was he who unlocked the problem so that the beautiful chapel became ecumenical in its widest sense. It's good to be in touch with God!

During the early 1980s, at the time of unrest throughout Britain in racially sensitive areas, it was fairly evident that Moss Side might also suffer. Bradford, Birmingham and Toxteth in Liverpool had all kicked off big-time and one could feel the tension in the air in south Manchester. The lads had heard that milkmen were not getting the empty bottles back from the doorsteps; also, that there were a number of youths walking home with new baseball bats which were being made in a local youth club. Trouble was imminent and we were powerless to prevent the inevitable.

At 3.10 a.m., that early July morning in 1981, my wife woke first when the phone rang. As I stirred, I heard her say, 'Well, put it on again.' It was Sergeant David Batty, night duty station officer at Moss Side who had announced to Chris that 'the wheel had come off'!

I took the phone and heard that hoards of youths were starting fires in various locations and then stoning the fire brigade when their engines arrived.

'OK,' I said. 'I'll be with you as soon as I can.'

'Sir,' said Sergeant Batty, 'don't come up Princess Parkway – you may get lynched!'

So, with little time to dress properly but thirty minutes to pray in the car, I drove in through Sale and Stretford.

The duty officer had called for assistance from other divisions which were prepared for this eventuality. A number of police vans with a dozen or so officers in each were now doing all they could to disperse the crowds, but not before the cycle shop in Princess Parkway was torched. Mr Roberts, who lived alone above the store, had managed to escape without injury but the shop, which had been in his family for three generations, was gutted. I went out in a van to see what was going on. For the time being, the youths had dispersed and the firefighters were at last safe to do their duty – but stretched to the limit.

Back at the station, I had enough detail to put into a detailed report for the boss and the Chief Constable;

Albert Leach arrived at about 7.30 a.m. having heard the news on his radio, and toured the area with me. The night duty relief had gone home to bed but the early turn lads were reporting a strong rumour that the police station would be bombed that night. I knew about a drugs raid and arrests at the north of the ground near the canal and that was being blamed by some – and, of course, in the media, exaggerated – though it was later recognised that so few knew about the raid it probably was not the trigger. Other factors showed that preparations had been made in the weeks before the rioting with the bats, and bottles to make petrol bombs.

I took the rumour of the possible attack on the police station seriously and, with Albert Leach, quickly made plans, one of which was to ensure that as few officers as possible were in the station and so would be deployed at other locations. By doing this we could ensure that they would be on the alert to rescue the station, rather than being trapped inside. Officers due for night duty were contacted to report for duty at 8 p.m. and I briefed about a dozen inspectors at 7 p.m. at Platt Lane Divisional HQ. I had already decided that my Chief Inspector would look after the station during the day and I would deal with the nights – for however long the rioting went on.

By 8.30 p.m., there was tension in the air as I walked into the station from a quick tour of Moss Side. There were only ten of us still in the station. Patrols in the streets had not detected anything disturbing except that there were very few people about. But the tension was tangible.

I had a constable at the top of the fire brigade training tower and at about 8.45 p.m. he radioed the station to say that youths were scurrying here and there, coming from all directions but going east, bypassing the station.

Ten minutes later, he radioed again.

'They're coming. Hundreds of them . . . bats, torches, all sorts of other weapons . . .' and his voice tailed off.

We waited for the onslaught. At the moment of the very first brick crashing through the glass front door, one of my officers appeared at the rear door with an insensible drunk who he had found lying in a gutter.

Sergeant Batty – back on duty after a day's sleep, unlike me! – was flabbergasted. With help, he searched the drunk, and three officers carried the man to a cell and locked the door. Then the fun began.

Bricks, wood, petrol bombs – and panic from one of my constables. We were repelling borders, dealing with the missiles, but he was rooted to the spot, speechless except for his sobbing. Then he started to cry out, shouting at his colleagues, at me and anyone he could think of, for getting him into this mess. I tried, in the middle of the chaos, to calm him down, but he was undermining the confidence of us all; so, to bring him to his senses, I grabbed him by his tie – and punched him.

He sank to the floor, eyes rolling. I thought, 'This is unreal.' I was still encouraging the others while this young man lay on the floor. I was anxious in case he was really hurt but after a few moments, he came to and stood up, eyeing me all the time.

'I'm sorry, sir,' he said, at last. 'I couldn't help it. I'll be all right. Where do you want me?' And he willingly soon joined in our fight against the rioters.

We gave the impression, by running here and there, opening and shutting doors, that there were more police inside the building than the ten of us; but imagine it: glass shattering all around us, not only the windows but internally in the corridors; acrid smoke billowing everywhere, darkness, all lights were out; throwing rioters out of the ground-floor windows; outside in the yard, vehicles under fire, the hollering of raving rioters. It seemed endless, until help came from the police vans. Then the other fight began between police officers and lawless youths.

Sometime later, on a search through the wrecked police station, we found a canteen assistant upstairs, frightened out of her life – and a Detective Chief Superintendent who'd sheltered under a desk on the top floor, grumbling about his suit being ruined. All ten of us who 'held the fort' were injured in some way or another but none seriously. There was an eerie silence as we crept through the mess and crunched on broken glass; the police vans drove away and then the TV cameras arrived. I was glad of that because at last we had some light! Reporters came in ones and twos; then Chief Constable Jim Anderton drove up and, typically, his concern was not so much for the state of the building as for my officers' welfare.

I gave an impromptu press conference, still in my torn and dirty uniform, outside what had once been the front door of the station. I asked the press to speak to my colleagues so that they could give their impression of the night's events and Mr Anderton was brilliant in front of the cameras.

Dawn had now come and in the debris-strewn front office, Sergeant David Batty, dirty and drawn, suddenly yelled, 'The drunk!'

Normally, an insensible drunk is visited in the cell every fifteen minutes, to look after their welfare; none of us had given the man a thought during our war-torn night. Sergeant Batty volunteered to open up the cell and we heard him trying to wake the unfortunate man. In a few moments, the two of them appeared and I don't know who looked the scruffiest. Sergeant Batty couldn't find the charge book so the drunk's property, such as it was – and still in the top drawer of the station office desk – was given back. He was escorted out through the rear (now wrecked) door and into the yard, with all the splintered glass, charred vehicles, bricks, sticks and debris.

'You gave us some trouble last night,' David said.

The drunk turned to him, eyes bulging. 'Did *I* do all that?'

The riots continued for another two days and police were in the forefront; national and local newscasters with banner headlines had many quotes from local people and outsiders who blamed police for the eruption. When Toxteth died down somewhat, Greater Manchester could have a high number of its police – who had been assisting Merseyside – back on home ground, and eventually the disorder fizzled out. The aftermath was bittersweet. Local householders applauded my colleagues; I went with my community contact inspector, Joe Rigby, into some of the clubs to listen to punters, and while some were fairly critical, they actually were the exception.

There was an official enquiry but some crucial people who had roles in the community of varying importance were not there to give evidence – which could have been decisive. I was invited by the chair of the Ministers' Fraternal – a group of pastors, vicars, rectors and priests who regularly met together – to listen to and answer their questions. I readily accepted because I felt that the policing viewpoint was not being sought. When I arrived at the church hall a little early, I stood in the foyer with no one to greet me but it gave me the opportunity to quietly listen to what were evidently preliminaries being discussed before the main agenda items. I was amazed to hear that it was a debate considering whether they should open the meeting in prayer because they had a police officer attending. And the conclusion? No, they shouldn't and wouldn't.

'Well,' I muttered under my breath, 'if you won't pray, I will.' And I did.

I was asked to sit at the front with the chair, facing a larger audience than I had expected. I was introduced and then the chair opened the discussion by vehemently condemning policing in Moss Side; that triggered a number of other clerics to continue the same line. There was very little attempt to try to understand the police, let alone give any kind of praise. I was being harangued. I waited for fifty minutes and then the chair, the vicar of the church nearest to the police station, gave me leave to speak.

I began in a deliberately quiet voice to try to gain some attention, only to find that I was being loudly heckled from all quarters. The chair did seek order once or twice and so I was permitted to have my say. I sincerely apologised to the people of Moss Side if it was felt that police action was heavy-handed and ill-conceived. I reiterated the framed quotation on my office wall, which I had learnt by heart on my very first day as a police officer:

> The primary object of an efficient police is the prevention of crime;
> the next, that of detection and punishment of offenders if crime is committed.
> To these ends all efforts of police must be directed.
> The protection of life and property, the preservation of public tranquillity
> and the absence of crime will alone prove whether those efforts have been successful
> and whether the objects for which the police were appointed have been attained.
>
> *(Sir Richard Maine, 1829)*

Something else I learnt and expounded to the Fraternal was that to attain these objects, much depends on the approval and cooperation of the public and these have always been determined by the degree of esteem and respect in which the police are held. Police officers should always remember that it is their duty to protect and help members of the public no less than to bring offenders to justice and that, therefore, police officers are servants and guardians of law-abiding citizens irrespective of race, colour, creed or social position, with unfailing patience and courtesy.

I knew from my perambulations and speaking to local residents at their gateways, at school parents' evenings and at some public meetings, as well as in local churches, that the law-abiding people were fed up with any sort of crime – theft, drug dealing and abuse especially. I recognised that some arrests looked harsh; that was the case when any suspect put up a fight.

After speaking and fielding many questions, I knew I was on the losing side. There were maybe three or four of the number who wanted to support local police and encourage them in their duties but sadly, most of these learned brethren of the Church – in hospitality, in language and accusation – were not very reverend.

I returned to my office subdued but with a determination to underline the message on my wall even more. As soon as I'd sat down the telephone rang and it was my friend, Father Leigh.

'You had a tough time this morning, didn't you?' he said. 'I think you and I know what the root cause of Moss Side's problems is – sin! I wonder if I might come to see you and see if we can explore a way forward.'

And that was the beginning of a real turning point in Moss Side.

18.

Vision and courage

Father Leigh arrived the next day and we talked and prayed for vision and courage. He suggested that we invite others who he knew would be supportive of a stronger link between the police and the public, and so began a series of meetings with two others (local black pastors) primarily for prayer and then for planning. Eventually, out of this, came three memorable things:

1. The group suggested changing the name of Moss Side Police Station to Greenheys. This was passed on to the Chief Constable and ultimately it became accepted by the Police Committee – the idea was take away any slur that might be accompanying the name 'Moss Side Police Station' and underline the new or reinforced lead of community policing.
2. There would be a much more clearly defined link with community groups, not only by the community contact section but by all police working in the area. This meant a thorough briefing and even training of our own staff but also of the Traffic Unit which, while not under my control, often worked in the district and the central CID whose enquiries would also impinge into the area.

3. The establishment of 'The Open Door'. Using the burnt-out four-storey former cycle shop, it became the centre of interest as a coffee shop, a second-hand goods store and distributor; it had two furnished apartments for those who found themselves temporarily homeless, and a social room. This was staffed by local volunteers and always a police officer as part of their duty. It became a focal point of the area and, as I understand it, an example which has been followed in many other inner-city areas.

I suppose there was even a fourth idea which came from this – I was invited regularly to speak and/or preach at some local churches where a police officer would not have normally been welcomed. *Strangely*, I was never invited to the established churches!

Another thing which came from the aftermath of the riots was a strong link with Manchester University. Some of my colleagues and I were regularly invited to Freshers' Week and asked to mingle with the new students, to talk about the area and convey to them the need for vigilance. One of the pieces of advice that we gave was for the girls to get themselves a boyfriend who would walk them to and from their digs or, if that were not feasible, to go about in large groups looking after each other. This introduction week began friendships between students and young officers so that there was much interaction between them at university social events, and those that we held in Greenheys Police Station.

Obviously, I was intent on healing the breaches of confidence that were a result of the disturbances. I knew three people who were at the heart of the young community and who might be able to influence the future. One of these was taken seriously ill at the end of that year and, when I heard he was in hospital, I went incognito to visit him. The Sister of the ward asked me not to stay too long and she drew curtains round the bed. I spoke to this sick man but he turned over, away from me. Again I spoke, trying to show some friendship but he didn't want to know. I left him a handwritten note of conciliation but heard no more. Very sadly, he who could have been a key to new beginnings died soon after, very prematurely.

Another of the respected leaders, who attended a local church, was willing to talk but, like his minister, insisted that he would never be seen at the police station or in my company. With the minister, it was a case of him cycling to Longsight, out of the immediate area, and me in scruffy clothes meeting to talk with him in the library. It was a similar situation with the other man, but we met in the back room of a doctor's surgery, again out of Moss Side. We made little progress.

I had made appointments to meet the third man but he had never kept one of them. After a while, I heard that he had begun to go to church. Then, the rumour was that Charlie Moore had become a Christian. And so it was; his secretary at Moss Side Youth Club had invited him to church on more than one occasion and eventually he succumbed. In weeks, he was convicted of his sin, sought forgiveness from the Lord Jesus and was born again.

Just after I had heard about this, he called at the station counter and asked to see me. I was in my office and was informed of his visit by telephone.

The sergeant said, 'Would you like someone to be with you? I'll get the duty officer to come in.'

'No. I'll come down and bring him up to my office,' I said. 'We'll be alone.'

'Sir, is that wise? You know he was behind the riots.'

'Yes, I know and I want to meet him – alone please.'

I went to the counter and put out my hand to Charlie. He seemed shy, but he shook it. I invited him upstairs into my office, and asked for a tray of tea.

'I hear good things about you, Charlie,' I said. 'What's happened?'

'I've changed,' he said. 'I'm a Christian now.' He was very nervous but he said he had come to say sorry about his behaviour, the incitement and the riots. Very seriously, and with some tears, he told me about how he came to faith in Jesus. His past had caught up with him and he had many regrets. But he recognised that Jesus had died for him and he could be forgiven.

It took some time for him to tell me this. Then I stood up and said to him, 'Have you ever hugged a honkey? Come here.' And we embraced till it hurt – a big, beefy Afro-Caribbean and an equally big British guy.

I hadn't seen my clerk, Bob, come in with the tea. But I believe he was quite shaken to see the perpetrator of Moss Side riots in a clinch with his boss.

'Can you forgive me?' Charlie asked.

I smiled as I told him I'd never thought this day would come. But he'd been given new life as a Christian, and was forgiven by God.

'Of *course* I forgive you.'

Charlie told me about the help that his local church had been when he had just not wanted to be seen there, especially after his part in the rioting. His approval and encouragement of rioting youths, their damage and violence, their anti-police taunting and the terrorising of a normally happy Moss Side was now behind him. Perhaps the most touching moment was when he asked, 'May I call you Robin?'

'Yes,' I said. 'Of course.'

I believe those momentous minutes together were the final link in a chain of new goodwill; this was strengthened even more when, after an invitation, I went to speak at his church. The pastor met me at the door as I arrived and said that he had a surprise for me – after the service. I finished preaching after several shouts of 'say it again, brother' and applause and cheering. I met a few joyful people on the way out, but then the pastor invited me into the vestry.

Standing there were three youths aged perhaps eighteen or nineteen; hefty lads, looking quite sheepish and not able to look me in the eye. The pastor intro-duced them – they were the leaders in the assault on the police station and threw the first bricks through the front door and windows. They were also members of Charlie's youth club but on seeing his dramatic change in life, had started to come to church – really it was back to church for their parents used to bring them when they were younger – and now had become Christians. What a life-changing God we know! This was an exciting part of the riot aftermath which the media, strangely, didn't pick up. I wonder why?

Charlie joined the group of ministers who regularly met in my office praying and planning the steps forward for this broken district. He became a real motivator and was the physical drive behind the refurbishment of the former Roberts' cycle shop which had been burnt out in the riots. It was Charlie who first suggested the idea of changing the name of our police station to Greenheys . . . and that was approved by all the hierarchy. Because he was so well known – as was his incredible change of lifestyle – he was at the forefront of many of the new ideas which began to change attitudes and even policing methods.

One would think that the job of a Superintendent was largely management and administrative. However, I was determined that I would keep my policeman's feet on the ground for as long as I could by being thoroughly involved in the daily tasks on the beat, without interfering with the inspectors or sergeants. I frequently reminded them that I had no problem with being telephoned at home or, by letting the station know my movements, being called wherever I was.

Of course, we had to get the damaged police station up and going again. The Surveyors' Department came and boarded up all the broken windows – only two were unbroken, on the top floor – so it made the building very dark and we were working under artificial light continuously. We wanted to make it attractive on the outside and experimented with large tubs of flowers, which, miraculously were untouched for the rest of that summer and I persisted with headquarters that we needed repairs to windows, doors and walls – all of which were desecrated during the siege. Remembering that my predecessor had been shot at (the bullet hole had remained unrepaired), I requested bullet-proof glass for the station. Although there was extra expense, it was eventually approved and, three months after the siege, the glaziers arrived. Several men were working on the station but had almost completed the ground floor when they arrived at my office. The two men said it would probably take the morning and into the early afternoon to complete my room so I used the time to patrol the area and make some visits.

I returned for lunch at the station and went into my office where the final window was being put in place. I watched as they fitted the window and then picked up a hammer from their bag.

'What do you want done?' one of them asked.

'You watch,' I replied. 'I want to see if this really is bullet-proof.'

I lunged at the side of a window hoping that it wouldn't even mark it; but the hammer smashed right through, shattering the glass. My clerks ran in to see what had happened but only saw the red faces of two workmen, and me glowering at them.

I asked the glaziers to cease work and spoke to our Surveyors' Department by telephone. A visit from one of them later in the day, and the testing of the already fitted glass, confirmed it – the glass certainly wasn't bullet-proof.

So, out came those fitted windows, back went the boards and we had another long wait. I was told that it will take some weeks as the glass had to be specially ordered but a week or so before Christmas, now five months since the disturbances, the glaziers returned.

One of them came to my office. 'Here's my hammer. Before we start, would you like to come to the yard and test the glass again?'

So I went armed with the hammer to the cheers of a few officers and civilians who were going to be spectators to this smashing event.

Crash! I hit the glass hard, twice, but only made a small mark.

'OK,' I said, handing back the hammer. 'It's all yours. A drink for all you workmen if you finish by Christmas.'

They worked very hard and on Christmas Eve morning, the foreman poked his head round my door.

'I think you owe us a drink.'

That wasn't the last of it, though; the glaziers had used putty to fit the glass and this ate into the material. It would, it was said, eventually dislodge all the windows in the station. So it started all over again. Thank God for a hammer.

Shortly after all the trouble, a complaint was made against two of my better officers that they had 'planted' petrol bombs in the rear of a van being driven by two local youths. The vehicle itself was stolen from

Wythenshawe, south of Manchester, and stopped by my vigilant officers in Princess Road, Moss Side. The youths had made a run for it and were both caught by the same officers about half a mile away. The allegation was that because the van had been left unattended while the chase was on, other officers had taken the van to the police station where previously prepared petrol bombs were placed inside. The complaint was made at the youths' first appearance in court, and the allegation was difficult to prove either way. Both officers, and the station staff on duty at the time were interviewed separately but concurrently and they were all adamant that there was no 'plant'. At the second hearing, I was called to the Magistrates Court to say what was being done about the complaint. I had to explain that at present it was an impasse but was then given the information, while in court, that the complaint now included me for 'authorising the plant'!

Charlie Moore called me before the next hearing for a private meeting. In my office, he took time to explain that the complaint had been a deliberate attempt to undermine policing in Moss Side and was a story wholly concocted by the two youths who had been arrested. Charlie had heard about it, thought he believed the youths and, because of our new relationship, was reluctant to say anything in case the allegations were true. It was Charlie who solved the issue when he overheard other young people congratulating the arrested youths for causing this unrest, doubt about policing, and the mammoth investigation. Charlie then confronted the youths and they knew then that they had been rumbled and confessed to him.

Eventually they appeared at Crown Court in Manchester. My evidence was short though I had a grilling about policing, criticising our methods in Moss Side, before the judge intervened. Eventually the youths were found guilty, including the extra charge of 'wasting police time' and they were sentenced to a period of youth custody. The judge called me back.

'Mr Oake, please convey to your colleagues that there is absolutely no stain on their character and that they all acted in the best traditions of policing. Thank you.'

Yes, a policeman's lot is *still* a happy one.

19.

An unusual call out

While I often walked the streets in uniform to keep up with the 'feel' of Moss Side, most of my operational exploits were following 'call outs'. One night, following a late meeting at which I was the speaker, I arrived home in Timperley rather tired. Chris and I had our time of prayer together and switched off the light at just past midnight. At about 3 a.m. the phone's piercing ring woke us and a sergeant's voice said, 'Sorry to wake you, sir, but we have some apes which have escaped.'

Apes? I thought it was a practical joke and I *could* have said 'You're drunk' but said instead, 'What do you mean, apes have escaped?'

'Sir, we believe these are dangerous animals and we need you to authorise firearms in case we need to kill them.'

I couldn't remember this scenario from any book I'd read. 'I'll come in – where are the apes?' I dressed quickly and drove fairly fast to Alexandra Road South where I arrived to see police cars, standing floodlights from a Traffic Patrol vehicle, 'Road Closed' signs some distance from the actual location, old people in dressing gowns standing on balconies and on the front lawn of an Old

People's Home, and police officers going from door to door waking house after house to encourage each of them to close all windows.

The duty officer greeted me; he was a level-headed character with a wonderful laconic style. Nothing worried him, even escaped apes. Without a smile and in a very matter-of-fact way, he told me that two men, entertainers by profession, lived together in a caravan and allowed their house to be overrun by monkeys and apes. One of the men had been away in Malta on an engagement but had stayed on with a new-found friend and was long overdue. The partner, taking umbrage, was alleged to have 'allowed' the animals free run into the garden, and a female white ape (about four foot six inches tall) with one of her young had escaped and was lurking in gardens behind the houses. Rumour from neighbours had it that the female was aggressive.

As I was listening to the inspector, a Dog Van screeched to a halt next to us – it was Constable Tony Collier with his normally very agile and effective German shepherd, Zack. Tony was a first-class handler. He listened in to our conversation.

'Leave it with me, boss,' he said, confidently. What he *meant* was 'Leave it to the *dog*'!

Tony Collier went to his van and, after a lengthy struggle, put on (or 'climbed into') the 'rabies' suit which all dog vans should carry. I don't think Zack had ever seen his master in such a contraption. The dog, tied by his leash to the wing-mirror of the dog van, stared, open-jawed. He started to howl like a ghoul, and growl, and then turned and tugged until the wing-mirror was pulled off. Zack hared away from Tony and leapt the back gate, trailing the damaged mirror. He disappeared into the darkness, where we thought the apes might be. The handler, furious and embarrassed, also tried to leap the gate but his 'suit of armour' prevented that. He tried to open it but the catch was rusted solid so with a waddle towards the gate – the top of which was just below his groin – and with a groan, and cheers from the aged spectators and colleagues alike, he toppled over it.

With much grunting and clinging to the tree next to where he landed, he got to his feet and disappeared in the same direction as his dog.

'Sir,' said the duty officer, straight-faced, 'have I your permission to call out a firearms officer?'

'Not yet. I haven't even seen a monkey, let alone an ape.'

'Sir, I assure you there is an angry ape . . .' He was interrupted by a howl, a strange eerie sort of choking and barking rolled into one, and then the dog appeared, leaping the gate from the darkness trailing a long leash and a wing-mirror. That there was an ape or something similar in someone's back garden I now had no doubt.

'Call him out,' I ordered, 'the firearms guy – now!'

'Right, sir.'

In my heart I knew I didn't want the ape shot and killed but I had to be prepared to have it brought down if it escaped into the road.

By now we had quite an audience, adults and children peering out of their back windows overlooking the gardens, though what they could have seen through trees and shrubs I could not think. Despite the time, nearly 4 a.m., a number of cars and taxis had stopped in Alexandra Road to see what was going on. Of course, the press had arrived and it wasn't long before two TV crews were on the scene. Their attention was suddenly drawn to Tony Collier looking like the Michelin Man, trying to get out of the garden gate. He waddled towards it, tipped over out on to the pavement, and his laughing colleagues picked him up. He struggled to get himself out of the suit which he knew he had to do to have any hope of retrieving his 'obedient' dog.

He called, he whistled, but there was no sign of a police dog, especially one that had howled in fright at the sight of an angry ape. Then we heard the faint but increasing sound of a wing-mirror – how it remained on the end of the leash after its adventures I'll never know – scraping on the asphalt as the dog appeared again; perhaps, I thought, Zack would be relieved to get back to normality with his handler in uniform and properly dressed. But no, the dog ignored Tony and leapt into the rear of the mirror-less dog van and kept its head down.

The clamouring media was enjoying the fun but, of course, this was potentially a serious incident. As I spoke with the reporters there was a shout in unison from those who could see: 'There it is!' Suddenly, the white ape emerged from cover with a smaller version behind it. The ape was not daunted by the crowd. *I* was the one who was daunted because here I was in the back garden – with the ape. Cameras clicked and there was much noisy excitement from all around, but no one dared go near the animal.

Then there was a message from Moss Side: 'Have tried several zoos and vets in the north-west; only two replied but will not attend.'

I got one of the lads to radio back to the police station my insistence that a zoo or a vet should be roused so that we could speak to a keeper about the ape – how dangerous was it? Was it precious? My instinct said that I must not have the ape shot but darted so that it could be captured alive.

I was surprised to see a car approaching at this point; it had come through the 'Road Closed' sign. It pulled up beside the uniformed duty officer and a little man with a pencil moustache jumped out.

'I am a lion tamer,' he announced, in a high-pitched voice. 'I heard about this on the news. If the apes are still in the garden, leave them to me.' He nodded, confidently. 'Animals respect me!'

The duty officer shrugged his shoulders, and glanced at me. I thought I detected a smile forming on his lips. I studied the little man. He didn't look like a lion tamer, in his pullover, trousers and running shoes. Well . . . what did we have to lose?

'Why not?' I said.

The little man elegantly leapt the garden gate and ran off into the bushes. The elderly folk cheered him on, and then there was a quiet murmur of expectation.

Then we heard a cry: 'Whoah! Get off!' followed by a loud scream. The 'lion tamer' cleared the gate very impressively, and cowered behind me.

'Sorry about that. She was vicious.' He muttered, 'I wonder if I should've worn my leopard skin leotard . . .'

I don't know how I didn't burst out laughing.

I had other – more conventional – offers of help from excited spectators (goodness knows what bare hands could have done) as I went to the front garden to inspect the caravan, which had bedding in it, but also stacks of bananas, many of which were decomposing.

The co-owner was standing nearby, smoking a hand-rolled cigarette. He seemed proud of the fuss he had created.

He apologised to me but added, 'The mother is very angry, probably frightened, and with her offspring is very, very aggressive. You must get hold of it sooner rather than later.'

Me get hold of it! I went with the man to inspect the house, the front door of which looked like any other in the road and was secure. I wondered which of the monkeys read the post which came through the letter box!

The back door had what can only be described as a mammoth cat-flap big enough for a tiger. The mess surrounding it – on the door and on the passage outside – was appalling. What is amazing is that none of us, not even the constable on the beat, had any idea about the property until that night. But with our torches we saw a number of smallish monkeys sitting on windowsills watching with evident glee as we wondered what to do next. We didn't know if any had escaped with the apes but the neighbour who first saw the white ape with its young said he hadn't seen any other animals bounding about.

I said to this owner of monkeys, 'Why don't you entice the apes with bananas? Surely they'd follow you?'

'What? There's no way I'm going near them after you lot have frightened them!'

The white ape glared at us, daring us to come near until, out of the early morning mist, a large red fire engine appeared, complete with extendable ladders. The station officer jumped down and saw me in the garden facing the animal. He didn't approach me; he called me to the pavement to talk!

'We heard about this from one of the boys who came in for a drink; thought these ladders might help.'

'Well, thanks. What do you intend to do? Extend the ladder over the garden and hope that the apes will cling to it, or will one of you go in and extend a hand to the apes from the ladder?'

Yes, I was being facetious. Still, not being able to think of a serious way the firefighters could coax an angry ape into its cage, I let them return to the station. As they left, I had a radio message that someone at Keighley Zoo in Yorkshire – and that's not just down the road – was on his way with a dart-gun, but it would probably be about two hours before he could get to us.

With that, we deployed our officers to tell the house-holders the news. I went to the Old People's Home where the only one properly dressed was the night duty warden. I apologised for all the noise and lights.

'That's all right. It's the best entertainment we've had for years,' she said. Just as she finished speaking, a police van arrived with eight (yes, eight) fully kitted armed police officers who piled out and stood in two rows like soldiers on parade.

A sergeant with them said, 'I'm not sure what this is about, sir, but no one seems to be taking cover. Is there a gunman in the vicinity?'

'Sarge,' I said, 'wrong information. We have an escaped female white ape and her young. She is apparently aggressive and all I wanted was a gun nearby in case the ape came out from the gardens.'

'An *ape*?' I've never seen a police sergeant more surprised. He pulled himself together and went on, seriously, 'So where do you want us, sir?'

'Sarge, I don't *need* eight guns,' I said, rather wearily. 'So deploy one gunman to walk with the duty officer here and keep the others in the van, please.'

This was overheard by the warden and some of the residents of the Old People's Home. Immediately I was at the centre of their wrath because they didn't want the ape shot! The press also began to take a deeper interest when they saw the firearms so that was another barrage of questions to field. Who'd be a Superintendent?

I was trying to think through, with my colleagues, what to do about the rush hour – the first bus would be coming through at 5.50 a.m – when the milkman turned up.

'I've been a ranger,' he told us, cheerfully, 'in Africa.'

I eyed him.

'I know everything about apes.'

'Oh?'

'I'll give it a bottle of milk,' he said.

I nearly said, 'Would you like a saucer?' but restrained myself.

'Milk? Apes don't drink milk,' said the monkey owner, scathingly. 'Only water. And they eat bananas.'

I had gathered that already and nearly said so.

Following the intrusion of the milkman, we decided to fully open the road while the ape was contained in the garden so traffic started flowing. But, as is often the case, the speed of traffic was slow as drivers were inquisitive as to why there was so much police activity. There were two minor accidents when drivers were not looking where they were going.

Finally, at 8.25 a.m., the vet arrived. He was one of those very clever men who like to talk themselves through what they intend to do.

'Erm, white apes; Madagascar? I wonder; yes, could be dangerous; about 150 lbs; I wonder if it has eaten . . . with young, yes, probably aggressive. Not too much sedative. Could dart from gate but better inside to be accurate. Yes, not too much . . . OK, get ready, chaps, she might dance a little before falling.'

And with that, he shot two darts into the mother and reloaded with something much smaller, and darted the young one. There was a growl, a flailing and a slight movement towards the vet, and then the mother keeled over. The young one simply rolled to the ground unconscious.

Cautiously, the vet moved towards the animals.

'What do you want to do with them?' he asked.

Very wisely, the duty officer suggested that he spoke with the owner who had gone into his caravan, and also asked him to inspect the house where the apes and other monkeys were roaming. It didn't take the vet long to condemn the conditions and, for a man who had displayed such a quiet disposition, let fly at the owner with very strong verbal language. In his fury, he wrote out a form declaring the premises to be unsuitable. He then said to me, 'I've condemned this house for the keeping of any animals but we only have about two hours maximum to get the apes moved.'

The saga ended at about 9.45 a.m. with the arrival of a large unmarked removal lorry with several cages on board. It loaded the two dormant apes, and then, with the helpful assistance of the owner who was now very remorseful, rounded up and caged the other inquisitive monkeys in the house and took all the animals to a local zoo.

I arrived back at the station tired and yet still chuckling, and heard something that made me laugh all the more. The normally affable Sergeant Parr had been the station officer. About five minutes before the ape incident, an older constable had radioed in that he had 'two cows in Alexandra Road North; van please for the prisoners'. He wanted a van for two prostitutes he had arrested. Then came the call, 'two apes escaped in Alexandra Road South'.

'What?' the sergeant had exclaimed. 'Don't take the mickey out of me!'

20.

Pole-axed

During our time in Manchester, Chris, the children and I attended, and were very much involved in, Altrincham Baptist Church where Dr Paul Beasley-Murray was pastor and his wife Caroline a great support. While there, she took an external law degree and ultimately became the Coroner for Essex.

Sadly, there was nothing outside of Sunday school for those under fourteen and so Sue was very disappointed that she couldn't join in with her brother and Judi. She and some of her friends persuaded Chris and me to think through the possibility of establishing a younger group and we talked this out with some good friends, Professor Harold Jones (dean of the Dentistry School in Manchester University) and his wife Anne. As we prayed about it, we four felt that we could meet the need and the day came when we advertised the new idea and a number of ten to thirteen-year-olds arrived at the Jones' house one Sunday evening. The children had the idea to call the group the 'Joakes', combining our surnames. We all had a good laugh but the name stuck. Sue, whose idea it was to start the Joakes, eventually became the group's leader.

My role in the church was that of evangelism and we had a continual ongoing series of outreach events, ranging from coffee mornings to men's breakfasts to ladies' afternoon teas. A number of non-church people came to these events and then to Sunday services; many of these were deliberately evangelistic. One great idea was the bi-monthly 'Face to Face' interviews, Parkinson-style, of well-known personalities who were overtly Christian. The first guest was Violet Carson, 'Ena Sharples' in Coronation Street. She put in our visitors' book, 'Here for grilling!' She was the forerunner of many celebrities who were open about their Christian faith and who came for an hour's 'grilling', touching many hearts and minds.

The Christian Police Association under the directorship of George Roberts in Leicester was also continuing to move forward, not only in the British Isles but furthering its outreach into Europe and many other places in the world. I had succeeded Jim Anderton as president, and was conscious of much prayer support. There were many opportunities to meet with other chief officers in the various forces, as well as having many invitations to take teams to preach at a number of churches and other venues.

One of the joys of being a senior officer in south Manchester was to fairly regularly meet His Royal Highness, the Duke of Edinburgh. As Chancellor of Salford University, his preferred means of travel was by helicopter and, because of the convenience in distance, the police sports ground at Hough End was used as a landing area. He was always polite and in a good mood and never without a quip or two about Manchester, the weather, the traffic and so on. Obviously, I tried to organise the quickest and safest route from the ground to Salford University and, on the first occasion, I had traffic temporarily stopped at large junctions to allow easy passage. When we arrived, the Duke said to me, 'Why hold up the traffic, Mr Oake? I am in plenty of time and you will have caused much frustration on the roads.'

I noted this for the next visit and, against my better judgment with royalty, escorted the Duke through Manchester's inner-city traffic which took several minutes longer than last time. At the university, the Duke said, 'Why the slow journey, Mr Oake? With a policeman at every junction we could've got here much earlier.'

On subsequent occasions, with that twinkle in his eye, the Duke would ask, 'Is it hold-ups and early, or the traffic and late?'

It was while at Greenheys that I was encouraged to apply for a place on the Senior Command course and went through the selection procedure in Eastbourne along with sixty or so other applicants – a three-day ordeal of written papers, intelligence tests, 'chairing' meetings and long interviews with chief officers. I also had an hour-long session with a psychologist. It was then that I was asked if a convicted murderer could ever be ordained into the Christian ministry.

'Yes,' I said, 'I believe it's possible.' And I went on to explain that anyone, however serious their crime, could receive forgiveness from God if they turned from their sin and trusted Jesus; he would make them a new person. From there we discussed whether *people* could forgive a murderer – for instance, a congregation.

'I wholly believe in the love of God through Christ who died,' I replied. 'Christians should forgive too.'

We talked more on this theme, and the psychologist then asked his final question.

'Would you yourself forgive a convicted murderer if he had killed someone close to you?'

'Yes,' I said. 'I believe I would.'

At that time, of course, I did not know I would be called upon to do just that.

I was one of thirteen selected and in the spring of 1983 reported to Bramshill Police College for the six-month course. It was demanding; hard work in a team or individually; visits to Miami Police Department, to the Avon & Somerset Constabulary, and the Metropolitan Police . . . each of these tasks to assist with problems which had been challenging the local personnel.

Towards the end of that course, I had a visit from Don Elliott, then Deputy Chief Constable of Greater Manchester Police and John Evans, Assistant Chief Constable (both of whom were later appointed as Chief Constable of the Devon and Cornwall Constabulary, John Evans following Don Elliott). They gave me the exciting news of promotion to Chief Superintendent and a return to police headquarters to take charge of the force Community Relations and Publicity Department. Along with that came the responsibilities in the Senior Officer's Mess, and becoming its president for two years. The Mess was a place of great camaraderie.

The shock of this new rank was quite challenging but not long after the appointment, I was pole-axed. At home, we had an integrated garage and, at the rear, the former and original garage for the property, which was used as a very spacy garden shed since a car couldn't access it. It was a prefabricated building but its roof crossbeams were fairly low and certainly below the six foot five inch headroom I needed. Although I had been in the garage many, many times, sometimes banging my head, I never felt it to be a particular threat. However, one evening, I went in to fetch some gardening tools, turned to come out but forgot to duck. At full speed, I cracked my head on a beam, was knocked unconscious and collapsed fully on my coccyx; Judi and Sue found me in a crumpled heap with a blue-grey egg rising on my forehead. I came round, feeling a little dizzy. Not wanting to make a fuss, I tried to get up but my legs wouldn't hold me. I knew I was concussed, but I also seemed to have little feeling in my legs. With my daughters' help, I crawled into the house – no more gardening that night. Judi must have thought 'not again' for the day after passing her driving test, I yelled for her to take me to Wythenshawe Hospital having severely slit my wrist on a broken piece of glass while I was building a greenhouse. She did well to get me to casualty before I bled to death.

Anyway, I found the numbness in my legs was slightly better the next day and I went to work, with Sue driving me into headquarters. But for the succeeding days, I had to recognise that something was really wrong as I just could not bear my weight for long when I stood up.

I phoned Freddie Griffiths, the Manchester City Football Club physiotherapist, who I knew well from my Moss Side days. He invited me to his rooms in St John Street. I was driven there by a colleague.

Following an extensive examination, Freddie said, 'Robin, this is not a minor matter and there's nothing wrong with your legs. You have a spinal injury which is beyond me. Hang on a minute.' He went next door to see Mr Peter Frank – the eminent and world-renowned orthopaedic surgeon – to see if he could fit me into his schedule there and then. Incredibly, for such a busy man, he did and I was helped upstairs to his consulting rooms and welcomed by his charming secretary. She said that Mr Frank would be a few minutes but meanwhile took my details and suggested that I undress to my underclothes. Soon Mr Frank came through the curtains and his 'What have we here?' meant me relating a summary of what had happened while he deftly fingered my spine.

Eventually, he said, 'You need two things – transport home and complete rest until I ring you to come to St Joseph's Hospital for surgery. You have a nasty injury which could have bad consequences for your career if you and I aren't careful.'

Within a week I underwent the spinal operation; Mr Frank visited me every day in hospital and then at home while I was convalescing. He and his secretary, Pauline, whom he later married, became firm friends of ours – a friendship which continues to this day. What a skilful surgeon; I have had no further problems with my back.

I was on sick leave for what seemed an interminably long time – in fact, it was only six weeks. My staff at headquarters were excellent and kept me up to speed with everyday matters while I had time to think about how much better our Community Contact Branch could be throughout Greater Manchester.

One of the changes I had thought through was to move our branch to the Lodge away from the main headquarters building, to encourage some of the more timid members of the public to come and see us without the palaver of getting through security. Another idea – not from me originally, but which was brought to me by my staff – was to build a boat. The vision was to get two professional boat-builders leading a team of ne'er-do-well youths to design and build a sailing vessel which eventually could be used to take young people on sea-faring trips to learn discipline and sailing expertise. It sounded like a good idea but needed a lot of thought and planning. A derelict warehouse near Openshaw, East Manchester was available though due for demolition; two master ship designers and builders were contacted and volunteered to give their time to such a project and it wasn't long before ten lads between sixteen and eighteen years old, all of whom had been in trouble with the police and were unemployed at the time, joined the project.

Throughout the planning, I had the job of finding the money; my hard-won budget was meant to be equally distributed between all fourteen divisions, and for us in headquarters too. We managed it partly because most of the lads came from a variety of areas and also because Jim Anderton and his team of senior officers were able to persuade the Police Committee that this venture would not only be good for the young people, but would reflect on the goodwill of the politicians in Greater Manchester.

21.

Chief officer status

It was a complete surprise to learn that the jovial but brilliant detective Charles Horan, Assistant Chief Constable (Crime), was to retire. He had spent his entire service career in Manchester – firstly with the Manchester City force and, on amalgamation with that and other forces, the Greater Manchester Police. Charles had been one of the Board members when I came for interview from London and had often taken the opportunity to give encouragement to my colleagues and me. His post was soon advertised in *Police Review*.

I felt that an application would be rather premature but counterbalanced that thought with the experience it would be to go through the interview procedures – even though this would be quite an ordeal. Some weeks later, I had the official letter from the Police Committee that I was on the shortlist. Amongst the other five was David Phillips, Chief Superintendent in the Lancashire Constabulary who had been a fellow student on the Senior Command course. He was a quality contender and some years later became the Chief Constable of Kent Constabulary.

The interviews, at County Hall, were over a period of three days – on the opening day, we had what we called the 'goldfish bowl'. The six of us sat in a circle with members of the Police Committee seated round us, the chair throwing subjects into the ring for open discussion by the candidates. It was to test our ability to debate, to take an opposing view, to not dominate the discussion and to be a good listener. Lunch was with the committee and we recognised then that our places at the table were pre-planned and that at every meal, we sat next to different members of the committee. Subsequently, each of us had to face the Finance Committee, the Community Relations Committee, the Personnel Committee, the Race Relations Committee, the Discipline Committee, the Crime Committee, the Operations Committee and finally, the Planning Committee. Each interview was about an hour in length, tiring enough for us as contenders but probably worse for the committee members!

We knew we were under close scrutiny and rightly so; the final hurdle was to be interviewed by the whole committee (all forty-five members), sitting in a 'horseshoe', with the chair, Mrs Gabrielle Cox, some twenty yards away, trying to control her members as they fired question after question. Sometimes, the members talked over each other – that might have been part of the plan to see how we coped and how we answered.

At the end of it all, we six men sat together in a lounge awaiting the outcome, the plan being that the successful candidate would be informed before leaving for home. An hour or so later – and without any awkwardness between us as we thought through the three days together – the door opened and Mrs Cox simply said, 'Mr Oake, please come with me.' My immediate thought was that this was an elimination procedure, that five of us would be called back to be told where we stood, and the final candidate would be informed of his success.

As we walked along the corridor, Mrs Cox whispered to me, 'Robin, you've got it but be surprised when you are officially told.' As we walked into the long room, I saw that Chief Constable Jim Anderton was there; he winked at me.

And so I was told, by Mrs Cox, 'Mr Oake, this has been arduous but profitable for us all but we are unanimous that you should be appointed Assistant Chief Constable. Congratulations and may you enjoy the new rank and position. Well done.' Members gave their approval and Jim Anderton was the first to come over and shake my hand.

This happened on a Friday and I was asked to be in post three days later on Monday morning! Jim had informed me that I would be in Charles Horan's former office and that I would head up the Community Relations Section, Press and Publicity and Force Inspectorate. So that Monday, I drove into work, with some trepidation; used, for the first time, the parking bay in the basement of headquarters now reserved for me and was whisked up to the eleventh floor to be greeted by my new colleagues and my secretary, who was as small as I was tall. My good friend, Deputy Chief Constable John Stalker, came along the corridor to shake my hand and take me into the morning session with the Chief Constable, to drink coffee and talk through the previous day or weekend with him to keep him up to date.

Sitting in my office some weeks later, Assistant Chief Constable (Personnel) Paul Whiteside walked in just before lunch and said, 'I've had a stimulating conversation with your son this morning, Robin.'

'Oh?' I replied. 'What's he been up to?'

'Didn't you know? He applied to join the Greater Manchester Police and was accepted. It was so good to talk with him.'

I knew nothing of this and in the evening telephoned to congratulate him. I asked why he hadn't told me of his application which must have gone in some weeks before.

'Dad,' he said, 'I wanted to know that I had done this off my own bat and, although I know that you wouldn't have influenced the panel, I just needed to be satisfied that I did it without you.'

I was absolutely thrilled, of course, that he had joined a superb organisation and had an interesting career ahead of him. I was a very proud father at the Passing-Out Parade at Bruche Police Training School, especially as I had been invited to be the inspecting officer, and took the final salute. My wife and I so enjoyed seeing our son, supported by Lesley, who was by then his wife, at the buffet afterwards, hearing his excitement about having done so well in his examinations and practical exercises. My son was a policeman! He was raring to go.

Some time later, I was speaking at a community meeting in Moss Side, and had an excellent reception and a good question and answer session. I had parked the car near Greenheys Police Station and, following the meeting, popped in to see which of my former colleagues was there on duty, hoping to join them for a cup of tea. As we reminisced and caught up with the news, in walked a sergeant – with Steve. Steve and I would normally have hugged each other but it didn't seem right with us both in uniform. He seemed stunned and later told me he didn't know whether to call me 'sir' or 'Dad'. I was unusually tongue-tied and it was the sergeant who broke the strange silence: 'Go on, Steve. Put a good word in for me!'

I next saw Steve on my way home from a late night at headquarters. As I drove down Withington Road, I saw a group of young people jostling with a police officer. I stopped a bit further on and dashed back. As I got near, I saw it was Steve – his helmet presumably knocked off in the fight. Then I noticed a police van parked at a junction. This made me realise that Steve was not alone as he was not a police driver yet. I felt that discretion was the better part of valour and drove away knowing that Steve would be very embarrassed if it was discovered that Dad had come to the rescue. He never knew what I had nearly done.

He later told my wife and me about an incident when he was a passenger in a police van in Chorlton. A young woman jumped into the road ahead of them as they were patrolling, waving frantically for them to stop. She came to the passenger door window and shouted, 'There's a headless man lying in the gutter round the corner. It's awful!' Steve got out and, while the van was being parked, looked where the woman was pointing. Sure enough, there was a body with one arm on the kerb and, yes, it was headless. As Steve walked towards it, the driver conspicuous by his absence (he said he was radioing for an ambulance!), he was feeling sick. Then the body moved. The man's head appeared and his other arm . . . from a drain, as he explained that he had dropped his car keys through the grille.

I found the Assistant Chief Constable's job very interesting and, of course, challenging. It was varied and involved much travelling throughout the Greater Manchester divisions as well as meetings with the Home Office in London, and speaking to other forces about our policies, aiming to have better links in relation to immigration, asylum seekers, and race relations issues.

One evening, I had come home from a particularly arduous day which concluded with addressing a public meeting in Wigan. The drive home took about an hour and I listened to the 11 o'clock news on the car radio. I picked up the following: 'Reports are being received of large-scale public disorder at the Golden Temple in Northern India. Some eye-witnesses have been speaking about gunfire and others mentioned serious injuries to many people . . .'

My mind began to race because of the possible reaction within our own Indian communities, and elsewhere in the country. When I arrived home, I asked our Information Room to alert all community contact inspectors, or their deputies, in the fourteen divisions, and ask them to be in my office by 8.30 a.m. next morning. I didn't get much sleep that night as I thought of possibilities of escalation and what we, as a police service, could do to alleviate the situation.

In my office the next morning we talked through the implications and ramifications of a spread of the Golden Temple disorder as the early morning news bulletins on radio and TV were revealing the feared escalation. My main question was to ask if our officers in divisions knew how to contact the appropriate Indian community leaders, and to await further advice once I had met with the Chief Constable and my colleagues.

At the 9.30 a.m. coffee meeting, I was immediately asked by Jim Anderton about the situation. Had I any plans? I mentioned my earlier meeting with the inspectors, and proposed that either he or I meet with Indian community or religious leaders from each division that very day and seek their opinions and advice. This was agreed and Jim asked me to conduct the meeting in our eleventh floor conference room.

My inspectors did an incredible job and, by 3 p.m., there were twenty-eight Indian leaders in the conference room. As I walked in there was a deathly hush and I suspected that there had been some argument and dissention before I arrived. However, one of the more elderly Indian gentlemen stood up after I had welcomed them and said an astonishing thing.

'Mr Oake, we hear that you are a man of prayer. We recognise that there are differences between us all here, but why don't you pray openly for this meeting?'

I was very surprised by this request as I knew that other faiths were represented in the room. However I did open the meeting in prayer and the discussion that followed was the obvious result. Yes, there were disagreements and opposing points of view but it was agreed that following our discussions, the group would meet again in three days after the leaders had returned to their communities with the purpose of defusing any anger or violence between different factions.

At the set time, we met again; I was asked once more to open in prayer, especially mentioning some of the leaders present who had relatives and friends involved in the skirmishes at the Golden Temple. Immediately after I sat down, the elderly gentleman who had originally asked me to pray stood up and crossed the room to another gentleman who I had noted had quite differing views; he rose and they hugged each other, which set up a train of hugs and reconciliation; many of the men were crying.

From that meeting came many positive suggestions which included communicating with Birmingham, Southall and Bradford (amongst others) communities so that there would be every effort to prevent any escalation in Britain. The Golden Temple disorder also ceased soon after that meeting.

I was very privileged after that to be welcomed at many Hindu and Sikh meetings in Greater Manchester. I usually attended with my local officers who, after all, had been the means by which these gentlemen had met together in police headquarters. The thrill of being a police officer at the heart of a peaceful solution!

My duties included being president of the Police Band and the Male Voice Choir; I enjoyed rehearsals and although the choir permitted me to join in with my bass voice I was never given the opportunity to play anything! Another of my tasks was president of the Police Sports and Social Club. I spent many hours at Hough End, the sports club headquarters. At the opening of a new sports hall extension, we had invited two professional basketball teams to play a game in front of the hundreds of police and families who had come for the occasion. Before the game, I was given a microphone and went on the court to thank the players and to introduce each of them – the incredible thing was that I was the shortest man on court. I cannot remember another occasion when I was the smallest man in a group.

At about his time, I had been to the Isle of Man twice, having been asked to speak at two Isle of Man for Christ crusade meetings – at Kirk Braddan, which must, at that time, have been the coldest church on the island or anywhere south of Greenland; and at the Corrin Hall, Peel – and had stayed with a lovely couple who have become good friends, Joan and Ken Quane. Chris came with me on the second visit and we were both struck by the beauty and magnificence of the island as we drove through the lanes, walked in the glens and visited castles.

The advertisement in *Police Review* for applications to fill the vacant post of Chief Constable on the Isle of Man did not initially attract us as a family but several senior police officers drew it to my attention. When I visited the Home Office, it was suggested that I apply for the post; it was said that should I be successful it would be helpful for me to try to persuade local politicians of the advantage in some criminal law being aligned with UK law; and, in addition, I might be able to bring some of the local police procedures into line.

I talked this out with Jim Anderton, who, I believe was not too keen on the idea at first but supported me when I eventually put in the application; I also spoke with Jim Brownlow who, while not discouraging me, warned me about being out on a limb and the difficulties of returning to the UK if I wanted to.

I sent in the application just before the time limit, feeling well qualified but quite open-minded that should I not be successful, that would be right in my Christian walk; if successful, then a new avenue would have opened. Chris was now very enthusiastic and the family all voiced their support.

I arrived on the island at Government Offices for the interview early in 1986 and discovered the three other candidates; the first interview – about two hours' long – was held in the Tynwald Room, jointly chaired by Dr Edgar Mann MHK and Noel Cringle MHK, the then Chairman of Home Affairs (lately, President of Tynwald). Members of the Department of Home Affairs made up the panel and their questions were searching; they sought my views of local and national policing and discovered that I had read much about the island prior to this interview. The issue of my Christian faith was raised, especially from Noel Cringle, a committed Christian. For the first time in my career, I was asked directly, 'Are you a Freemason or have you any connections with Freemasonry?' I was able to say an emphatic 'No' to both parts of the question. Incredibly, this point was brought out in a House of Keys debate in November 1990 about the judgment of senior government officers on the island. It was said then that the present Chief Constable was not a Freemason and, to many people, this enhanced his position.

The second stage was an interview at Government House with His Excellency, the Lieutenant Governor, Major General Laurence New (later Sir Laurence) whose grilling was even longer and deeper. But he also took time to speak of my being a Christian, and the part that this played in my public and private life.

Only a week later I was informed, firstly by telephone and then by formal letter, that I had been successful and that the appointment would commence on our twenty-fifth wedding anniversary.

22

Come over!

Just before I left Greater Manchester, our daughter Sue married David. We had a lovely time at the wedding reception at Hough End – a very fitting 'goodbye' to Manchester. That was Saturday 30 March; I was leaving on the 2.15 p.m. ferry from Heysham the next day, to start on the Isle of Man Constabulary as Chief Constable on Monday 1 April 1986.

I arrived on the island at 5.45 p.m. and easily found 16 Cronk-y-Thatcher; Barbara and Clarence Jefferies had offered me their empty bungalow until a permanent home could be found for us. Here I was on my special wedding anniversary and Chris was 100 miles away in Timperley! That evening I was visited by Mary and Michael Darnill who lived nearby. Mary mentioned her Christian beliefs, and we talked about our common faith. Then Michael remarked, 'Perhaps God has sent you to get me!'

Next morning – having unpacked the heavily laden car the night before – I left for police headquarters and was welcomed to my office by George Davies, the Deputy Chief Constable, at precisely 9 a.m. I had met George some three weeks before, along with my predecessor,

Frank Weedon, on a day trip. What I didn't know was that one of the constables – a member of the Christian Police Association – had supplied every police station and every office in HQ with a centre-page copy of my testimony from the CPA monthly magazine. I could feel the suspicion – perhaps even slight fear – what was this new chief going to be like, as an active and overt Christian?

Several people, colleagues, neighbours and others who I met, reminded me that I was now a 'come over', being non-Manx, and that I might one day become a 'BO' ('buried over') if I stayed. Most of them didn't know that my wife had deep connections with the Isle of Man being a Murray of Athol. In earlier years the Dukes of Athol were governors of the island. In fact, soon after we arrived, we were at dinner with Dick Gawne, a member of the Police Court Mission, when it was discovered that he was a cousin of Chris', he also being part of the Murray clan. Furthermore, her aunt had married into the Smelt family, and one of their predecessors was Governor of the island. So perhaps by proxy I might at least have a foothold.

My first week was spent with George, travelling through the island to different stations, or visiting offices. One of my first questions to officers was, 'Why are you doing that?' when I saw something different from what I had been used to seeing in England. The early replies were, 'Because we've always done it that way, sir.'

'But what is the reason for it?' I would persist.

Word got round pretty quickly – 'make sure you know why "we've always done it that way"'!

We agreed to have a morning meeting at 9.15 a.m. each weekday to keep us all up to date with what had been going on each twenty-four hours. That meeting was soon dubbed 'morning prayers' by the force.

At one of those meetings in early May, George asked me, 'Are you chairing the meeting tonight?'

'Which meeting is that?'

'The TT Marshals' meeting.'

The TT Marshals' meeting? I knew that TT was short for Tourist Trophy and referred to the annual two-week motorcycle race meeting which was held in late May and early June. But I wasn't aware of the meeting and said so. 'Why should I chair it?'

'Ah,' said George. 'Perhaps you haven't been told; you're the Chief Marshal!'

Well, I did chair the meeting with George, very magnanimously, sitting beside me keeping me on track. Being a sport lover, I began to relish the thought of the festival in a month's time.

The next surprise was being summoned to Government House to meet with His Excellency the Lieutenant Governor and the Royal Visit Committee to finalise details of the imminent visit of the Duke of Kent. My predecessor, Frank Weedon, had initially been on the committee. Prior to this meeting, I had had a harsh telephone call from a senior politician who requested – indeed, almost tried to order me – to tone down the police security, as too much money and staff were wasted on these royal visits! My polite response was that there was an accepted protocol with tried and tested procedures for the royal family's security and safety. While I accepted that the Isle of Man had many differences from the rest of the British Isles, I assured the speaker that I would stick to the plan until I saw a need for change. His response was irate and rude but my final comment was, 'If the Duke of Kent gets a hole in his head, who loses his job – you, sir, or me?'

When the TT arrived, I decided that to get to know the 37-and-three-quarter mile course, and to speak to marshals and my officers who were stationed at various points, I would walk the whole length, which meant walking about four miles a day in practice and during the racing. So I started out and enjoyed both the fresh air and the atmosphere. The constables and marshals were very surprised that the Chief Constable was walking! After escorting His Excellency, the Lieutenant Governor to the grandstand, the start-line formalities, speaking to various riders and being on the line to see the staggered start of all the riders in each race, I had ample time to drive to the point where I had reached the day before to continue the walk.

I was startled on one of the race days when, on walking in full uniform past the crowded bank at the then petrol filling station opposite the Beary Plantation and en route to Glen Helen, I heard the sound of machines which I mistook for the radio broadcast of the race. Having just acknowledged the marshals and the crowd, I turned in horror to see a sidecar outfit only fifty yards away and I was on the racing line since the pavement on the river bridge there was non-existent. I leapt over the bridge wall as the combination passed me at breakneck speed. I landed in the River Neb, safe, but soaked and embarrassed, especially as the crowd had seen it all. They cheered as I scrambled up the bank.

At one of the 'morning prayers', John Platt, Chief Inspector, asked if I intended to do the 'walk' again for the Manx Grand Prix, due in August.

'Yes,' I said.

'Sir, may I suggest that you walk the opposite way next time?' said John. 'At least you'll see what killed you!'

Following that 1986 TT meeting, I had linked up with 'Race Mission', a small band of motorcyclists who had a

Christian passion for riders and their families. Their tent was sited near the main paddock and was run by Pat Slinn, former (and still sought-after) mechanic to top riders and teams, and former racing star, Graham Bailey – a police sergeant from London who had made his name as a part-time racer on the circuits and on the Isle of Man. After the racing, while at the airport seeing Graham off, along with a journalist from *The Daily Telegraph*, we talked about Race Mission and the journalist reminded us of the open-air service which was once held in the field behind Braddan Church in the summer months. Why not reinstate a similar idea but hold it in the grandstand on 'Mad Sunday', the middle Sunday of the two-week meeting?

With that seed sown, the idea began to grow and so the next year, 1987, at the TT, the first of the open-air grandstand services – completely non-denominational – took place, conducted from the winner's rostrum with full cooperation from the authorities and public address facilities laid on. The services were normally conducted by the vicar of St Ninian's Church, not in any robes but wearing a leather jacket; participants to read, speak or conduct prayers were always taken from those thoroughly involved in the racing fraternity.

One top-ranking rider from New Zealand, a winner on three occasions, walked into the Race Mission tent to meet and apologise to Pat Slinn for the cynical way he had treated him and his team in years gone by. He confessed to becoming a Christian during the past year and then began a 'life-threatening' hug. The rider asked if he could participate in the 'Mad Sunday' service and, indeed, was interviewed on the rostrum which he had occupied officially in previous years as a former winner.

The TT was always a fun time but exhausting for the bobbies. We always prided ourselves that it was policed without the need to seek help from other police forces. However, after some discussion about the number of continental casualties on the roads during the festival, especially riders from Germany, we invited officers from the Motorcycle Department of Germany's traffic police to second three riders to the island; this proved to be a worthwhile exercise.

The behaviour of the fans was, if not faultless, pretty good and much fun was had during the evenings on Douglas Promenade with impromptu displays on bikes, Bushy's Marquee and perhaps the longest bar in the British Isles, and the funfair. There was tremendous bonhomie between the vast mix of cultures. One evening, in Bushy's tent, two of our attractive policewomen were mingling with the drinkers when five foreign leather-jackets began to argue with them about the long wait to purchase a drink. They then started to push the women around. Within a moment, the five guys were hoisted above shoulder-height by a number of fans nearby and taken across the Promenade. One by one they were thrown, fully clothed, into the sea as people cheered and chanted, 'Leave *our* police alone!'

Early on in my appointment on the Isle of Man, I used to walk through the Douglas streets and, indeed, Ramsey, Peel, Port Erin, Port St Mary and elsewhere on the island to familiarise myself with the geography, and also to meet colleagues and the local people. However, while off duty and shopping with my wife in Strand Street, Douglas, we met Inspector Joe Cook on duty and in his uniform. He came to speak with us and after a short conversation said to Chris, 'Have you heard that there is a shortage of valium in all our chemist shops due to police officers buying up stocks for fear of being spotted by the chief?'

I also spent time visiting various departments and was out one evening in a Traffic Patrol car driven by Terry Stephens. As we were approaching the main road south out of Douglas, a distinctive BMW flashed past the junction at high speed.

Terry looked at me. 'Shall we?'

'Yes. Go go go!'

We swung into the main road and, at the top of the hill, at the roundabout, the BMW, now some distance away, turned right. Terry had his foot hard down and we gradually closed the gap but it took some minutes before we got close enough to blue-light the driver so that he stopped.

Terry and I got out. The BMW driver had his window down and was recognised as Chinese.

'Sir,' said Terry, 'you were driving very fast in this built up area. We found it difficult to catch up with you.'

The driver beamed at us and said in broken English, 'Can goo much fasser; you wanna see me?'

'But,' said Terry, pleasantly, 'you see, there is a speed limit . . .'

'But no thees car! It ca goo much fasser; no leemit on eet.'

I turned away at this point. It was difficult to keep a straight face. 'Thank you, sir,' said Terry, at last. 'Just be careful in future, please.'

On another occasion I had an informal visit to the Prosecutions Department to find that the officers were out and the civilian support staff were holding fort. I asked where everyone was and they told me about enquiries being carried out – also, one of them was prosecuting in the High Bailiff's Court in Douglas. So I popped down and quietly walked in through a rear door only for the then High Bailiff, His Honour Henry

Callow, to stop proceedings and for the court to rise to its feet.

The High Bailiff addressed the court. 'It is so good to have a visit from the Chief Constable. Sir, you are very welcome. With your permission, may we continue, please?'

A police officer was continuing his evidence in the witness box when the defendant, who I didn't recognise, suddenly stood up, pointed at me (now sitting down in the public seats), and shouted, 'That's the man who put me here! It's his fault I'm in the dock. He grassed on me!'

I was stunned. Then I remembered. My wife and I had hosted a small dinner party at our home and two of our guests were Robin and Dandy Bigland from St Johns. Robin had left his car outside in the road with the lights on but the battery had drained and he couldn't start it. I volunteered to take the couple home and, as we approached their house, our progress was blocked by a car in the middle of the narrow road, lights blazing and the driver's door left open. We noticed that a man was relieving himself in the Bigland's gateway. On seeing my car, the man staggered to his vehicle and drove off. It looked as if the driver had had a few too many and I radioed its registration number to Police Information Room for circulation and, if possible, to stop the car and speak with the driver.

The car was stopped about eight miles away. The driver was arrested and later charged with driving while over the limit. And the court case was being heard when I walked in. What a coincidence.

The High Bailiff showed some sympathy for the driver because of this. The driver 'addressed' the bench quite loudly about how unfair this was and that it was a conspiracy. I was a little red-faced, I believe.

Still, following the evidence, to which he had pleaded guilty anyway, it was announced to the court that the man had three previous convictions for drink-driving and other motoring offences – so his heavy fine and long ban did not need too much sympathy after all.

My philosophy for command was not to be a boss issuing orders, demanding obedience and respect, blaming others for mistakes, being authoritarian and evoking fear. I had learnt that the best way forward was certainly to be a leader, but to seek to encourage respect and support for one another; leading the force by listening, having an open-door policy and by cooperating with our politicians, councillors and commissioners. The Isle of Man Constabulary was a comparatively small – but very busy – police unit and was much more effective in its policing by operating as one large family with mutual support, rather than having men and women driven from above, causing resentment and misunderstandings. It was, in those days, a very happy and efficient force, certainly fully supported by its Police Committee and by the general and law-abiding public. The sense of privilege by being its Chief Constable grew as the years went by.

I was determined that policing and community should dovetail at all ranks and I know the force was already, largely, adept at that. I encouraged all to be at agricultural shows, local events such as fetes and garden parties, and even to attend commissioners' (local council) meetings. I found myself being asked to open various events and to speak at Women's Institutes, Catholic guilds, men's breakfasts and so on, and was very glad to do so.

Early on, I went to open a garden party in Lezayre, in the north of the island. As we arrived, my wife was taken aside and asked (she told me afterwards) if I had a sense of humour. The chairman began to introduce me and made one or two wisecracks about the name Oake; as he did, the Ramsey Town Band began to play 'Tie a Yellow Ribbon Round the Old Oak Tree' which prompted two elegant young ladies to start running round me on the platform completely binding me with – yes – yellow ribbons. When they had finished, to the cheers of the large and appreciative crowd, the band then started up with 'Hearts of Oak'.

So, here I was, unable to move, being asked to open the party! I am rarely stuck for words but this nearly floored me. I think I said a few witty things and, as I was speaking, the young ladies came and untied me. I declared the party open and then was presented with a dainty oak tree in a flower pot; I planted it in my garden, smiling as I did so. The tree – now quite mature – remains.

Earlier in this chapter, I mentioned the Darnills; sadly, their son was drowned that summer on the Norfolk Broads. We had already made arrangements with the Darnills to holiday together in Tenerife and, while we were there, we all attended a 'church service' in a hotel and had lunch together. Conversation naturally went to the loss of their son; then, Michael suddenly asked, 'How do I become a Christian?' We talked at length before Michael prayed out loud to ask for Christ's forgiveness and invite him into his life. So maybe God did send me to 'get' him after all.

23.

'He has been so good . . .'

Early on after my appointment, I was approached by a posse of officers in the social club – 'The Office' – to ask if I would sanction a monthly in-house magazine which would be informative, hopefully contain some hilarity and, maybe, points of law and so on. It was open to anyone to contribute an article, anecdote or cartoon. I discovered that the editor would be Inspector Dudley Butt. The idea was worked on once I gave my approval in principle, and given the title *Screeyn Naigit* (Manx for 'news'). Following a weekly soccer programme known as Saint and Greavesy (former players Ian St John and Jimmy Greaves), some wag on the production team devised another Saint and Greavesy in the centre pages of the magazine and it always depicted some anecdote which involved Alan Greaves of Traffic Patrol and the chief. Some of the 'incidents' were apocryphal but hugely popular and very humorous; others were based on truth, albeit somewhat embellished.

One report which was actually true involved the two of us; I had asked the control room to have a car pick me up at headquarters at 11.15 a.m. to take me to a meeting with the chief minister, which would be followed by lunch. I loathe being late at any appointment and had expected that fifteen minutes to drive to Government Offices about ten minutes away would be ample. I waited until gone 11.15 a.m. and went into control to ask who was picking me up.

'Alan Greaves, sir.'

'Please ask where he is and ask him to step on it.'

I heard his reply on the radio that he had been on the mountain road and was held up. Now 'on way'. Indeed, at just gone 11.25 a.m., the car screeched to a halt at HQ steps, tyres smoking, driver steaming! I jumped in but Greavesy was in a stew, couldn't stop apologising, and drove the car as if we were at Le Mans.

At St Ninian's traffic lights, a busy four-road junction, there was a loud crash, and flying metal in front of us as three cars piled into each other, blocking everything. Alan Greaves leant across me, took hold of the radio mike and with the button pressed down for the whole force to hear, he yelled at me, 'Sir, this is a job for a real policeman! You'd better get out and walk while I clear up the mess.'

That story took up the whole two centre pages.

Once, I was driving home, off duty, with my wife through Ballasalla. I saw ahead of me the English registration Volvo 760 Estate which was on loan to the force for a trial. A police officer was standing by it.

As I drew up, I saw it was Alan Greaves. When he saw me, he became highly agitated.

I got out of my car, concerned. 'What's the problem? Can I do anything?' I was thinking that there was an escaped prisoner, a robbery or that maybe Alan was in the middle of surveillance.

'Oh, no,' groaned Greavesy, 'it had to be you, sir; the car's run out of petrol!'

Yes, you've guessed. Centre page again. Apparently Greavesy had been involved in a chase that had gone on for so long and at such a very high speed that Alan's fuel gauge eventually registered zero. Then the getaway car stopped to help to siphon petrol – but zoomed away when the 'Saint' arrived. Hmmm. Not quite as I remember it!

Of course, there were serious moments too, when there was no time for humour. It was about 11.15 p.m. on 1 July and I was about to get in the bath when the phone rang and Detective Chief Inspector Neil Kinrade asked to see me immediately. He gave no indication of what it was about but arrived around twenty-five minutes later. Without going into too much detail, he told me of information received from the Royal Ulster Constabulary. It was possible that three men, known to have terrorist connections, had boarded a fishing vessel in Northern Ireland. Word was that they were heading for the Isle of Man. He and I knew that the Parachute Regiment was on the island, enjoying some rest and recuperation from their tour of duty in Londonderry. We knew they could be possible targets. The Regiment was to be on duty forming the guard of honour on 5 July, Tynwald Day, when crowds would be at St Johns for this great day of pageantry and reading of the law.

Having got this and other more precise detail from Neil, I asked him to return to headquarters, alert the coastguard ('already done' he said), get the team ready to begin complete surveillance, and await further instructions. I then had no option but to telephone the chief minister, Miles Walker, who was in bed; I went to see him and alert him to the news. I advised him that confidentiality was essential and that I needed his authority to contact the cabinet office in London as I thought it wise to have military input and intelligence. Also, while the Council of Ministers should be informed, the media should not until it was clear that the suspected terrorists had landed and that we had discovered where they were. And then, when the military personnel arrived and my surveillance team was deployed, we should discuss wider publicity and eventually hold a press conference. I didn't want to have the islanders unnecessarily in fear.

The military arrived early next morning and I informed the chief minister who had already called an emergency meeting of Comin (the Council of Ministers). I now knew that three suspects had landed and were probably in the north of the island (as was Jurby Camp where the Parachute Regiment was barracked). While I knew there were advantages on an island – even one as big as the Isle of Man – when it came to pinning down hidden suspects, there were a million and one places to lie low. However the constabulary on the island knew more about the crevices and dark places than any strangers up to no good.

While I was briefing the military and the chief minister I had word of a stolen car in Ramsey; then of a garage attendant in Ballaugh who was suspicious of two Irishmen in a car which he thought he recognised as someone else's. The attendant didn't know about the possibility of terrorists, but he telephoned Ramsey Police Station and it was enough to mobilise our all-island road hunt, using every vehicle and motorcycle we had. The vehicle was spotted through Foxdale and then as it sped past a junction at Round Table. Actually the vehicle was stopped on the lower Sloc Road not 100 yards from my house though I was in Douglas police headquarters at the time. My police officers were very subtle and very brave in both stopping the car and arresting the men. After all, they had no idea as to whether the suspects were armed or whether there were explosives in the car.

That wasn't the end of the matter; a third suspect was still at large and all drains, gulleys, bridges and indeed, any other crevice where explosives could be hidden, had to be thoroughly searched and then sealed before Tynwald Day. The Parachute Regiment had been alerted and their commanding officer offered to help in the search. But the chief minister, the military and I felt it was too big a risk to allow them out of barracks.

Information reached my Special Branch that the third suspect had fled the island in an unknown boat and he was arrested on 4 July in Bradford.

It was a tense week but the Tynwald ceremony went without a hitch. And I feel the island should be eternally grateful to God for deliverance from the loss of life and dramatic tragedy and disaster which might have been.

Her Majesty the Queen and the Duke of Edinburgh arrived for, amongst other engagements, Tynwald Day and I was in the line-up at Ronaldsway Airport.

The Duke looked at me rather quizzically. 'Not you again, Mr Oake. How's the traffic today?'

Another 'not you again' came from Her Royal Highness, Princess Margaret who arrived at Ronaldsway for a four-day visit. I was, as was customary, in the line-up to welcome her. The Princess looked up at me and, as she shook my hand, she said, 'Not you again, Mr Oake. Where have you been?' I hadn't seen her since my days at Rochester Row in London. The formalities concluded, she came back to me while her car was waiting and asked if it were possible for me to arrange for a stone of queenies – small shellfish similar to, but not related to, scallops – and a stone of Manx kippers to be placed on the Royal flight in four days' time to take back with her.

'Leave it with me, ma'am,' I was glad to say.

Chris had met the Princess at Government House but when, the next day, Her Royal Highness alighted from her helicopter at Cregneish – a living museum in the south of the island – there was Chris with my mother, who then lived with us. Mother had never met any of the royal family and asked if she might come to the village to see the Princess. Princess Margaret spotted Chris and came across the road and said exactly what could be predicted, 'Not you again, Mrs Oake.' Of course, my mother was delighted when introduced to Her Royal Highness and said to Chris afterwards, 'Is Princess Margaret an old friend of yours?'

Princess Margaret had a busy schedule during the first three days of her visit and on the fourth, Tynwald Day, I arrived at Government House with the cars for procession. Her Royal Highness made a beeline for me.

'Good morning, Mr Oake,' she whispered. 'I take it my queenies and kippers are ready?'

'Yes, ma'am, they are on the plane.'

'Thank you so much. But my lady-in-waiting has asked if she, too, might have some queenies and kippers to take back. Is that possible, please?'

'Ma'am, this is a public holiday,' I said, 'and it may be difficult . . . but even if we have to fish for them ourselves, I will do my very best.'

In the car, I asked Inspector Jim Kelly to put out a general call regarding the fish. And so began a very interesting and unusual dialogue over police radio: 'Tell the chief I think I have a contact . . . Heard the message and can complete' and later, after the Tynwald ceremony, 'Mission complete. Royal plane stocked.'

However, as we approached the airport gate, another voice crackled over the radio: 'I have the requested items! What do you want me to do with them?'

Jim Kelly looked at me. 'Ooops.'

I shook my head. 'Tell him to deliver them to police headquarters, traffic office . . . and say how grateful I am.'

Princess Margaret and her lady-in-waiting were delighted with their fish – and we, later, at headquarters, were also delighted as we shared out our unexpected spoils. The bill for the royal fish was sent to Government House, but I had no option but to pay for the 'extras' . . . still, who cares; they were excellent.

Chris and I have been highly privileged to attend two Buckingham Palace garden parties – once when I was Assistant Chief Constable in Manchester and then again, as Chief Constable Isle of Man. On that second occasion, we were able to meet and talk briefly with Her Majesty the Queen. Then the late Princess Diana spotted the cap badge with its three legs of Man and came to speak with us. She wanted to know what else happened on the island apart from the well-publicised motorcycle racing. We mentioned many other events but she took a real interest in the World Tin-Bath Championships held every summer in Castletown Harbour, and organised by members of the Campaign for Real Ale. The Princess began to giggle at the thought of the spills and thrills and asked if it would be possible for her to be invited – even to participate! She giggled again, hand to her mouth as if to say, 'What am I doing?'

Sadly, I could never explore that possibility.

Once, when Her Majesty and Prince Philip came to the island in the Royal Yacht *Britannia*, Chris and I were very privileged to be invited for dinner along with dignitaries. We were really surprised and delighted.

Britannia was anchored in Douglas Bay. During pre-dinner drinks, we were introduced to Prince Andrew and the Duchess of York, with whom we still correspond today. After dinner, we stood on deck to watch the firework display on Douglas Promenade. I was standing next to the Duke of Edinburgh for a while. He asked me how long I had been on the island and if I enjoyed it – 'Surely, there's not much to do here after Manchester, is there?' – and then remarked, 'You never gave me a firework display like this at Hough End!'

The Royal Yacht came to the island, briefly, twice more before its decommissioning: firstly, to disembark Her Majesty the Queen, who was on board travelling to Scotland for her annual holiday, but interrupting the trip to meet the Duke of Edinburgh and Prince Edward (who had arrived overnight) prior to flying to Belgium for the funeral of King Baudouin; then, secondly, Prince Charles arrived to fulfil some official engagements, and Chris and I were on board again by invitation for afternoon tea on the foredeck. While we were conversing with two First Lieutenants who were involved in a kind of naval Christian Union on board, Prince Charles asked about our own Christian experience and encouraged his officers by saying how much he appreciated their witness and prayers.

On this trip, Prince Charles was visiting Ballakermeen High School. John Platt (later my deputy) as Chief Inspector CID and therefore in charge of security, was travelling with me in the front car of the motorcade. Following the visit, John jumped into our car while it was moving once he saw that 'the principal' was in his vehicle. He mistimed it. As he went to get in the rear nearside door, he caught his foot and off came his shoe. Nevertheless, he got in, furious at the driver for speeding off so quickly. He only had one shoe now, and we couldn't stop.

On arrival at Government House, I left John in the car as I wanted to escort the Prince in.

Then Prince Charles handed me a shoe.

'I believe this belongs to your Chief Inspector. You ought to have him properly dressed on these royal visits!'

A question was raised nationally about the cost to police of royal visits and, indeed, another chief constable actually asked his Police Committee to intervene, requesting no more royalty in that particular year; his budget could not stand the expense. As a direct result of that, a number of chief constables, including me, invited to Buckingham Palace to discuss together, with Prince Charles and Princess Anne, any ways of reducing the costs without compromising safety and timings.

It was a very useful debate and in a final session we were talking freely and I asked Princess Anne, 'Ma'am, we welcomed you to the Isle of Man a few weeks ago. Your reason for coming was for a charitable purpose, "Riding for the Disabled". Would you object if on other less formal occasions, the local chief constable was in civilian clothes?'

The Princess immediately replied, with a straight face, 'Mr Oake, while I like to see you in uniform, you are much better undressed.'

We had a lovely visit from the Duchess of Kent; her primary task was to tour St Bridget's, our hospice and then she had two other engagements, one of which was to spend some time at a nearby residential home. As I was involved with Age Concern, I knew a number of residents at the Homes on the island so, with the Duchess touring with the staff, I went to visit an elderly lady I had known for some time. Sadly, she wasn't very well and very disappointed not to be meeting the Duchess in the lounge.

I knelt by the bed and spoke with her and she asked if I would pray for her. I was doing so when, very quietly, the Duchess herself walked in.

'Please carry on, Mr Oake,' she said, gently, 'I will join you.' And she knelt down taking the patient's other hand as we continued to pray.

The Duchess's comment as she rose to leave the room was, 'May God be with you – he has been so good to me.'

24.

Honoured

My involvement with the CPA continued throughout my term of office though I passed on the presidency early as I felt it right that a colleague from a Home Office police force would be far more accessible than I was.

There was no branch on the island when I arrived but I determined that we should not be lacking in this respect. I was careful to point out to colleagues that I was not keen on anyone joining the CPA just because I was involved – and I doubt that that ever was the case. Anyway, the branch was established in 1987; the inaugural meeting was chaired by His Excellency the Lieutenant Governor, and the First Deemster (island judge) His Honour Arthur Luft also attended with senior members of Tynwald, amongst others, in a crowded Central Methodist Church in Douglas.

I never wanted to preach at colleagues about my faith; I truly believe it is one's manner of life and attitude which either helps or hinders colleagues, or indeed anyone, to come to faith in Christ. I was delighted on the island to see police officers coming to such faith and others, whose faith was perhaps dormant, being enlivened so that their Christian life became vibrant again. To me it is a great joy to counsel anyone who is seeking Christ and I have had that privilege time and again at churches and chapels where I have had a part.

I was still able to get to CPA annual meetings, though not every year, and occasionally to council meetings; and, in my role as a Christian police officer, there were many opportunities to speak and preach on the island and abroad. Perhaps one of the most thrilling speaking engagements was when I was invited to the Festival of Evangelical Choirs at the Royal Albert Hall, to be the closing speaker. Frank Boggs was the soloist, and I was so glad to meet the man whose voice has long enthralled me on records.

Following the rehearsal with the magnificent massed choir, we were having refreshments backstage when a waitress said to Frank, 'Coffee, Mr Boggs?'

'No thanks,' he said, straight-faced, 'I'm a Christian.'

There was a moment's silence, then laughter.

Soon after this, there was an Isle of Man Newspapers Elegance vote for two men and two women; I didn't know of any entries but was ultra surprised when the result came out, not because of the other three winners, but because I was there! Ruth Anderson and Susan Watterson were the ladies voted for, and Miles Walker, Chief Minister, the other man. The accolade given me was that I was the only person who could make a common or garden police uniform look like a Jeff Banks designer suit. You see, policing is a real joy.

I love the game of golf and, since my early days at university, have played the game without much distinction but with great enthusiasm and enjoyment. I played in all ranks and on the Isle of Man was invited to join in with the Police Golf Society. The members asked me to be their president. I thought it went with the office but –

and I was naïve not to see this – it was really so we could have a President's Day where the president donated a trophy, bought and presented the prizes! I was invited to tee-off at The Manx Variety Club's 'Help to Help Others' International Charity Golf Classic at Rowany Golf Course under the scrutiny of both the island's leading golfers and many from the United Kingdom and even the continent, to be played over three days. I must admit to feeling daunted, almost like that feeling before going into court to give evidence. The moment came with a microphone introduction and, wonder of wonders, my drive went straight down the fairway. That was strange because I wasn't feeling too well having crashed my head, once again, on a beam while visiting the Costains, a local farming family. The concussion seemed to make me see double; so glad I hit the right ball.

Chris also enjoys sport as much as I do so for our annual holiday in 1990 we travelled to Auckland for the Commonwealth Games, staying with Police Commissioner John Jamieson and his wife Anne, good Christian friends of ours. Similarly, in 1994, we took summer leave to travel to Victoria, Vancouver Island, Canada, for the Games there.

I was involved primarily with the Games through my tiny but supremely efficient secretary, Diana Killey, whose husband Ron – a former international cycling ace – was secretary of the Commonwealth Games Association. Diana noted that I read the sports pages in newspapers and thus I was collared!

I was thrilled after this to be elected chair of the Commonwealth Games Association, Isle of Man. There was an immense amount of work to be done, and I enjoyed it; I also loved the travel. Each year, the General Assembly of the Commonwealth Games Federation is held in a different Commonwealth country and, sometimes, to coincide with the Olympic Games wherever they are held. Then there is the European Assembly, which meets twice a year, hosted by one of the European countries. I was very grateful for the opportunity given to me in this role and especially for the privilege of attending the Games – in Kuala Lumpur, Manchester and Melbourne – and to represent the island at various receptions, ceremonies and so on. I also participated in the medal ceremonies, hanging medals round the necks of world-class athletes.

But for all of this excitement, I have also had some down times. Once, I was in hospital as an in-patient, incarcerated for some seven weeks. I had kidney surgery which, in fact, necessitated four visits to the operating theatre. Following the final operation, I found eating quite difficult but one of the nurses recognised my plight.

As I sipped a little cold water, she said, 'Just shut your eyes for me, will you?' I thought she was going to give yet another injection but no. She continued, 'Just imagine your favourite food, where you last ate it and the taste of it.' I tried that and she said, 'Well, what was it?'

'Queenies.'

'OK, I'll go and speak to the chef and see if he can make that dish and then I want you to try to eat it.'

A little after lunchtime for the other patients, that same nurse came back. On her tray was a meal, with queenies in a scallop shell and cheese sauce with a little parsley. Unknown to her, I heaved when I saw it but the aroma from the dish made me sit up and at least try to eat. The first mouthful was difficult but it reached my tastebuds and I had another spoonful, then another.

'Please thank the chef for me,' I said to her.

'It'll do you good to go for a walk down the corridor, so why not thank him yourself?'

Later, she came to 'collect' me and accompany me to the kitchen. I was shuffling in my dressing gown and slippers and though I had combed my hair, I certainly didn't resemble a chief constable. My surprise when we opened the kitchen door to see the head chef and his staff lined up in their clean 'whites'. For a moment there was a pregnant pause then we all burst out laughing. The chef had imagined that I was on an official visit to the hospital, and had asked for queenies to sample the food! Anyway, he permitted me to 'inspect' his staff. It did me so much good to have a laugh. It was a good step forward to recovery.

While I was in hospital, despite my telling the Minister of Home Affairs, Eddie Lowey, that I was due for surgery, a rumour had sprung up that I had had an argument with a fellow golfer and had been struck with a three iron. As a result, my wife had left me and that I was resigning from the police force.

Without checking on any of this, a member of the House of Keys tabled a question to be answered by the Minister of Home Affairs, 'Is the personal behaviour and professional judgment of the Chief Constable a matter presently under consideration by your department?'

There was no debate; the late John Corrin, MHK made a long speech based on the rumour and the minister replied in no uncertain terms that there was no injury, Mrs Oake and the chief were still together and he was not resigning. Mr Corrin was howled down by nearly all the MHKs present.

When my wife arrived to see me in hospital following the Question Time, which she heard – and of which I have a full copy – the Sister of the ward asked why she was there.

'Haven't you left your husband?' she asked.

'Ah,' said Chris, 'I've heard that; but where have I gone?'

I suppose in a small community, this sort of thing is inevitable, but with a lively sense of humour, I was able to see the funny side.

Within a year of my arrival on the Isle of Man, I was contacted by the then chair of the St John Ambulance and invited to be a member of the Council. I had been involved with the Ambulance since 1957 while in London and later in Manchester so to have this continuous participation was a thrill. This led, later, to my being invited to take the role of Commander. This added a further burden in one sense but the busyness of the role was exciting and made a strong connection between police and young people (Badgers and Cadets), and adult volunteers, and linked with the increasingly popular first-aid training for the business community. The role of Commander led on to my being asked to become a member of Chapter – the central committee in London. The Order of St John is a Christian organisation and it was a delight to have this involvement with so many people who sacrificed much time in leading, training and going out on duty. It was such a surprise to be given the accolade of Knight of Grace and Justice within the Order of St John; to meet and talk with Nelson Mandela, similarly promoted, at the Investiture at St James' Palace by the Grand Prior, the Duke of Gloucester. I was very grateful to Garter, King of Arms, who designed my Coat of Arms; I supplied the three-word motto – and what else could have been chosen? 'More than Conquerors' which spoke for the family.

This honour, I believe, belongs not to me but to my whole family and also, of course, to St John Ambulance on the Isle of Man, whose tireless work by senior volunteers and those in the office should never be taken for granted.

I was invited, too, to be part of the original team when
Age Concern (Isle of Man) was established, and somehow ended up as its chair. This charity was linked with
Age Concern, England, but in fact was entirely independent on the island. What a privilege to have my
small part as a Trustee. I was also a committee member,
representing the Isle of Man Constabulary, of the
Association of Airport and Seaport Police; another
involvement outside of the police service was with the
Alcohol Advisory Service.

We used to attend Broadway Baptist Church but it was
fourteen miles from where we lived so that wasn't helpful for any midweek activities or evangelistic work. I
talked this over with David Gordon, the pastor, and he
agreed that we should start to pray this through for it
affected a number of people who travelled in from the
south.

One day I was out walking when it seemed that God
was putting something into my mind. What about merg-
ing with the few members of the Christian Brethren,
meeting in the old Wesleyan church in Port St Mary?
David and I talked, and went to see Will Payne, the senior elder there, one Thursday. After we had spoken
about our thoughts, he stopped us.

We expected a rebuff but he said, 'The Holy Spirit has
sent you here tonight. We are having two days of prayer
and fasting because tomorrow we have to respond to
Shoprite who have offered £125,000 for the premises. We
thought we could meet in someone's home as there are
so few of us, and the money would go to the Lord's
work – but this is the right answer.'

Shoprite's offer was declined and it was not long
before details of a new Trust were settled. The new Port
St Mary Baptist Church was duly established with about

twenty-five members. My initial involvement as chair of
the Trustees was to oversee day-to-day pastoral work,
the finances, the outreach and to preach too. A leadership team was moulded together and, two years later,
we appointed Reverend Tom Owens as part-time pastor.
His expository ministry was so appreciated but, sadly,
he died with cancer, very prematurely. When a full-time
pastor, Reverend Jonathan Stanfield was appointed
some months later, the leadership took over much of the
Trustees work and I took a less prominent role. The fellowship is well over 300 and now another site has been
established for those members who travel from anywhere north of Ballasalla. God's working here has been
truly amazing.

Obviously, I had been used to being accountable to the
people of Greater Manchester and thereby scrutinised
by the Police Committee and, often, other councillors in
the various capacities. I knew that politics were different
on the Isle of Man especially since there were no party
politics, at least for elected members of the House of
Keys or members of the Legislative Council. As with
forces across the UK, the ultimate authority for policing
– and indeed, the prison, the probation service and the
fire brigade – is the Department of Home Affairs. On the
Isle of Man, the current incumbent Minister of Home
Affairs assumes the role of Chairman of the Police
Committee and he will have a number of others alongside – Members of the House of Keys principally and
other community representatives. I believe it is only
right that policing is fully accountable in this way and I
never found it uncomfortable, even though there were
some disagreements and long debates. But I was a little
taken aback when, for a period, I was expected to attend
Government Offices, with the Minister of Home Affairs,

to face any politician who cared to turn up and, under the chairmanship of the Speaker, to take questions once a month. It was entirely unscripted and most of the questions were about incidents I may never have heard of – or perhaps had heard a whisper, but didn't know all the facts. Not only was this daunting but I recognised that much of what was said to me was hearsay from a third party and nearly always inaccurate.

However, on one occasion, I was accused of allowing prisoners to be unlawfully detained against their will, and of allowing my officers to be violent towards them and failing to give prisoners their rights. One of the members present then underlined this.

'Yes, when I was arrested, it was all I could do to stop myself being beaten to pulp. It was only the intervention of my lawyer which gave me protection.'

Afterwards the member said quietly to me, 'Robin, don't take this seriously; we were only trying to wind you up!'

At the end of each year I had to write the Annual Report of the previous twelve months, and present a business plan for the year ahead. I wrote it principally for the Minister of Home Affairs and Tynwald but wanted it readable for the whole island. It was usually full of good news. Though committed crime is never a happy subject, good detection rates are, and we had the accolade in the *Police Review* from Her Majesty's Inspector of Constabulary, Sir Geoffrey (now Lord) Dear: 'This is the highest detection rate in the British Isles' (*Police Review*, May 1995). A month later, from the Home Office came a league table of police forces, which took into account all manner of policing issues in relation to percentage of population. The Isle of Man was number one again, and had been for four years. I was privileged to be awarded the Queen's Police Medal for Meritorious Service, but dedicated it publicly to all who contributed to the making of this great police force. When I received the medal from Her Majesty the Queen at Buckingham Palace, her words were very complimentary. But I said, and I meant it, 'I don't deserve this, but the Isle of Man does.'

What an honour. How can I not conclude that being on the island meant that a policeman's lot – even at top level – was a happy and rewarding one indeed.

25.

Retirement

I enjoyed policing so much that retirement, although inevitable, was never something I looked forward to. However, we had completed a five-year reorganisation, and I gave twelve months notice of my intention to retire so that for a year I could oversee the changes; I could judge whether adjustments were necessary – and, of course, it gave time for the Police Committee and government to begin the search for a successor.

It was strange that all but one of the Police Committee pleaded with me to postpone my retirement – I was, by age, going three years prematurely – and a good number of politicians, civil servants and the community did all they could to make me stay on. It was tempting but Chris and I had prayed about this decision, and talked with close friends and the family, so that we had no doubt that it was the right time to hang up the uniform. Wonderfully, I was not in the least stressed, was fully fit and, in fact, planning to run the London Marathon the following April – which I did.

That final year seemed to go too quickly and, as the last day approached, in September, I sensed a doleful feeling in the staff. This was made worse for my secretary, Diane, who had been anticipating a hip operation (she had been island badminton champion in her younger days but had damaged her joints through so much sport) and said to me, 'Mr Oake I really don't want to work for anyone else. I think I will retire when you do.' That very evening, I had a telephone call to say that Diane had collapsed and died at home. What a dreadful shock for Arnie, her husband, and for us all. It was 1.30 a.m. when I arrived at the house, at the same time as the undertakers. The family asked me to participate at her funeral at Broadway Baptist Church, where I was able to speak of her Christian faith, her buoyancy, her abilities and her lovely family.

Shortly after this, I was attending a conference in Manchester about security in the north-west. It was attended by chief constables and assistant chief constables. My flight had been booked and I arrived at Manchester Airport on time. The stewardess opened the plane door after the engines had shut down and, as I got up to reach for my case, I suddenly saw my Special Branch son Steve at the front, talking to her. I saw her point down the plane. She then asked all passengers to take their seats immediately.

Steve came down the aisle and grabbed me in my seat, pulling me up to stand.

'Steve! What's – '

'Don't you "Steve" me. Come on out.'

I was dragged off the plane, much to the consternation of other passengers – and my embarrassment. As we got to the steps, the stewardess winked at me, which gave me the idea that this was a set-up.

Steve had a colleague at the bottom of the steps and the two of them frogmarched me into the Special Branch office in Terminal 3. As the door closed, he and his colleagues burst out laughing.

'Hi, Dad. Welcome to Manchester!'

Looking out of the window, I saw a police Range Rover draw up. Suddenly Steve and a colleague grabbed me again. I was pushed, roughly, into the rear seat of the police car in front of the passengers who were still disembarking from the plane. With a screech of tyres, I was driven away at speed . . . all the way to police headquarters.

My son phoned me that evening and said, 'Sorry, Dad. But what a laugh!' He had inherited my sense of fun.

I was being hounded by the media to see if there was a sinister reason for my early retirement. Early! OK, it was premature, as I have already mentioned, but I had completed forty-two years in the police. Of course there wasn't anything underlying my decision. I wanted to leave with the satisfaction of having proved, through all the stresses and strains of policing in all ranks, that Gilbert was completely wrong.

The force had a retirement party in The Office – where else? It was organised by that master of entertainment, Inspector Dudley Butt (now a member of the Legislative Council) who had invited such a number of guests that there was literally no room at the Inn. Most of the constabulary was there and the principal guest was my old pal, Norman Wisdom, who lived on the island. He welcomed me with open arms as I walked in to the crowded room.

'Hiya, Titch!' he yelled, and jumped into my arms.

It was a memorable evening; I was put in the dock, charged on two counts – with premeditated murder of the seriousness of policing, and fraudulently converting a miserable constabulary into one of humour and satisfaction. I wasn't allowed to plead.

A variety of 'witnesses' arrived to substantiate the charges, recalling incidents from the last thirteen years of policing. Of course, Norman played the fool all evening in a uniform five times too big for him and, with truncheon in hand, kept reminding me who was boss. This all went on well into the night, with one anecdote after another; a night of fun, a night when I deeply appreciated the loyalty, the industry and the humour of probably the finest police force in the British Isles.

The next evening a huge party was held at the Hilton Hotel and over two hundred attended. The buffet was enormous, but there was no top table so informality reigned. Alan Cretney, then my superb deputy, began to get anxious because many people were arriving who had not responded to their invites – they had just turned up – and some had heard about the party and hadn't known it was by invitation only.

I said, 'Let them in. When the food runs out we'll make another decision then.'

It's all decisions being a chief constable.

It was a little more formal than the night before! My whole family was there, from England and Wales. A number of impromptu speakers made some very complimentary comments, most of which were thoroughly undeserved, and I was given some magnificent gifts. People are so generous. We arrived home at 1.30 a.m. and I was awake again at 6.30 a.m. to have my Quiet Time of prayer and Bible-reading, and breakfast, so I'd be ready to leave home by 8 a.m. I wondered why Chris insisted on this – 'You mustn't be late on your last day' – though I had not been a police officer for so long without recognising that some conspiracy was afoot.

As I went to the door, suddenly blue lights were flashing, two-tone horns were blaring – outside, lined up, were four police motorcyclists and the Range Rover with Sergeant Ian Young driving and Inspector Carolyn Kinrade smiling away. Neighbours came out to see what was wrong and who was being arrested, only to see me climbing into the rear of the car.

Ian turned to me, as was customary at the beginning of a motorcade, and asked 'Any last instructions, sir?'

'Yes,' I said. 'We are sixteen miles from police head-quarters. It is now five past eight; I'll give you twenty minutes to get there, so I can be in my office by 8.30 a.m.'

He radioed the outriders. 'Fast one, lads.'

So we sped off to the loud cheers of neighbours, friends and family. All junctions were covered as the motor cyclists leapfrogged each other. We made the High Bailiff pull in to the kerb, I seem to remember. One of our church friends, whom Chris had 'tipped-off', deliberately ensured that he, too, would be called to pull in while he was driving to Douglas. No motorcade has gone through Quarterbridge's two roundabouts more efficiently than we did.

When I walked into my office, I found my desk swamped with papers and files covered in red 'Urgent' stickers. For a moment I thought the morning was spoilt – until I realised it was a ruse. The telephone kept ringing, too, as one colleague after another rang to say good bye.

I had to leave at 11.30 a.m. to catch my flight to Southampton – then on to Guernsey for a family holiday. I printed out a notice on my computer which said 'I am going out; I may be some time' and placed it on my strewn desk. My stand-in secretary, Nicki, came to me in tears and asked to say 'goodbye' in private. Then she led me out and, unknown to me, the civilian and police staff of headquarters had secreted themselves on both sides of the corridor, the stairs and foyer, to the police car which Carolyn was driving. I was so moved as everyone wanted a handshake or a kiss; in fact it took nearly twenty minutes to reach the street. I was so moved at this

unexpected and impromptu send-off and, amazingly, I
was there in time for the plane – though with an anxious
Chris waiting at Ronaldsway.

Goodbye police headquarters; goodbye policing. It had
had its difficult moments; it had had some very sad
times, nerve-racking times, rewarding times and exhilarating times. My overall picture however, Mr Gilbert,
was that my lot was – yes – it was a happy one. At the
end of it all, I could seriously thank God for calling me
into the police service, for the opportunities I had had to
serve him, as well as Her Majesty as Queen and Lord of
Man, for the enrichment of my Christian faith through
that service, and the fellowship of Christian colleagues
and the sheer joy of introducing many colleagues and
members of the public to a personal faith in my Saviour,
Jesus Christ. My walk in being a follower of Christ permeated my work and off-duty hours throughout the
forty-two years.

Thank God for it all.

Postscript

Many people have asked me since I left the police service if I miss it. Generally, my answer is that I don't miss policing, or the politics which accompany it, but yes, I do miss the camaraderie of colleagues. Policing was part of a wider family; no one was more or less important than anyone else. If that cement, binding colleagues together, is eroded, then morale, enthusiasm, loyalty to one another and efficiency begins to crumble so that ultimately, the rank structure becomes a hindrance and whoever is chief is isolated, having lost touch with people to whom police give service; civilian staff seek jobs elsewhere and officers only want to count the days they have left before retirement, or even resign to take other more satisfying jobs.

I did have two experiences soon after my retirement which, though they seem to be linked were actually completely unconnected. I was walking through Strand Street in Douglas having just completed another St John Ambulance First Aid refresher course. I am not good at remembering names and had noticed a grey-haired lady approaching me, probably fifty yards away. I thought I knew her but was searching my brain to think of her name. Suddenly she stopped, clutched her chest, leant against a shop window and slowly collapsed to the ground.

I rushed forward, immediately thinking of what it said in the St John manual about heart attacks. I knelt beside the lady, and felt her pulse, which was faint.

'Someone call an ambulance!' I shouted at the gathering crowd of shoppers, clamouring to see what had happened.

My first aid expertise was not all that good though I had just passed the test that morning, but I knew enough to see that the breathlessness and the weak pulse were an ominous sign. She was unconscious but began to stir and I tried to quietly ask her a question or two about pain. The lady, whose name I still couldn't remember, was partially deaf so I increased my volume. At this, she seemed to wake up.

'Are you Mr Oake?' she whispered.

'Yes, I am,' I replied.

'Oh! I thought you were dead! I'm seeing a ghost.'

Although she was taken to hospital as a precaution, in fact she hadn't had a cardiac arrest but had literally fainted with the shock of seeing me walking towards her. I didn't know I had that effect on ladies.

The other unrelated incident was a few weeks later. I was in my Commander's uniform of St John Ambulance and standing outside Marks and Spencer's with a collecting box. A number of people were very generous and most people said a few words of encouragement as they slotted in their coins and notes. Then a rather elegant lady who I don't think I had met before, saw my uniform and, because I suppose it does look a little like that of a senior police officer, said, as she put some money in the box, 'Ah, Mr Oake, I see you have been resurrected.'

Stephen

One final word concerns my son Stephen, and I finish where I began. Those who knew I was writing this book thought it might be a contradiction and tarnishing of my enjoyment because Steve followed me into policing, then ultimately lost his life while arresting a suspected terrorist in north Manchester.

I was so thrilled and proud that Steve had, as a Christian young man, felt called by God into the Greater Manchester Police. I was glad that he had done it on his own initiative and in collusion with Lesley and his family rather than involving me. I knew how much he thoroughly enjoyed his policing – on the beat, in Traffic Patrol and eventually in Special Branch, which was his real forte. We kept in close touch, of course, and shared many experiences. I was always glad to help where I could, give advice and encourage him.

Yes, it was a dreadful shock when he was murdered; it devastated the family for a while and also his many colleagues not only in Special Branch but in the wider force, and police officers throughout the country. Yet, as the Bible states, what man meant for evil, God has turned to good (see Gen. 50:20). Steve's courageous witness on and off duty was something to behold; he literally laid down his life for his friends. His sporting and musical talents were admired by many, especially when he and Lesley led worship at Poynton Baptist Church. His infectious humour still brings a smile to our faces. He was a character, full of fun and yet so serious about his work.

Steve's bravery at the scene of his death when, by his actions, although fatally stabbed, he protected his colleagues in the melee and thereby saved their lives – and also, prevented the proposed contamination by this terrorist group which could have poisoned and killed thousands of people. Steve was later honoured by Her Majesty with the Queen's Gallantry Medal and his actions have left a lasting testimony to his commitment to His Lord and to the people he served, of which we are all very proud. He has been remembered in a special way at the Greater Manchester Police Training School, Sedgeley Park, where the CID Wing has been named after him with the words, *'This Training Facility is dedicated to the memory of Detective Constable V07655 Stephen Robin Oake, loving father, husband and son, a committed Christian and Police Officer, who gave his life serving and protecting the public and colleagues.'*

Despite all this, I still believe that Gilbert was wrong, though constabulary duty in the nineteenth century could, possibly, be slightly different from that in the late twentieth and early twenty-first centuries. *This* policeman's lot is (and has been) a happy one!

If you would like to contact Robin Oake, you can write to him at

Robin Oake
c/o Authentic Media
9 Holdom Avenue
Bletchley
Milton Keynes
MK1 1QR
England

Index